Securing Pakistan's Tribal Belt

COUNCIL *on* FOREIGN RELATIONS

Center for Preventive Action

Daniel Markey
CSR No. 36, August 2008

Securing Pakistan's Tribal Belt

The Council on Foreign Relations is an independent, nonpartisan membership organization, think tank, and publisher dedicated to being a resource for its members, government officials, business executives, journalists, educators and students, civic and religious leaders, and other interested citizens in order to help them better understand the world and the foreign policy choices facing the United States and other countries. Founded in 1921, the Council carries out its mission by maintaining a diverse membership, with special programs to promote interest and develop expertise in the next generation of foreign policy leaders; convening meetings at its headquarters in New York and in Washington, DC, and other cities where senior government officials, members of Congress, global leaders, and prominent thinkers come together with Council members to discuss and debate major international issues; supporting a Studies Program that fosters independent research, enabling Council scholars to produce articles, reports, and books and hold roundtables that analyze foreign policy issues and make concrete policy recommendations; publishing *Foreign Affairs*, the preeminent journal on international affairs and U.S. foreign policy; sponsoring Independent Task Forces that produce reports with both findings and policy prescriptions on the most important foreign policy topics; and providing up-to-date information and analysis about world events and American foreign policy on its website, CFR.org.

The Council on Foreign Relations takes no institutional position on policy issues and has no affiliation with the U.S. government. All statements of fact and expressions of opinion contained in its publications are the sole responsibility of the author or authors.

Council Special Reports (CSRs) are concise policy briefs, produced to provide a rapid response to a developing crisis or contribute to the public's understanding of current policy dilemmas. CSRs are written by individual authors—who may be CFR fellows or acknowledged experts from outside the institution—in consultation with an advisory committee, and are intended to take sixty days from inception to publication. The committee serves as a sounding board and provides feedback on a draft report. It usually meets twice— once before a draft is written and once again when there is a draft for review; however, advisory committee members, unlike Task Force members, are not asked to sign off on the report or to otherwise endorse it. Once published, CSRs are posted on www.cfr.org.

For further information about CFR or this Special Report, please write to the Council on Foreign Relations, 58 East 68th Street, New York, NY 10065, or call the Communications office at 212-434-9888. Visit our website, CFR.org.

To submit a letter in response to a Council Special Report for publication on our website, CFR.org, you may send an email to CSReditor@cfr.org. Alternatively, letters may be mailed to us at: Publications Department, Council on Foreign Relations, 58 East 68th Street, New York, NY 10065. Letters should include the writer's name, postal address, and daytime phone number. Letters may be edited for length and clarity, and may be published online. Please do not send attachments. All letters become the property of the Council on Foreign Relations and will not be returned. We regret that, owing to the volume of correspondence, we cannot respond to every letter.

This report is printed on paper that is certified by SmartWood to the standards of the Forest Stewardship Council, which promotes environmentally responsible, socially beneficial, and economically viable management of the world's forests.

Contents

Foreword

Pakistan constitutes one of the most important and difficult challenges facing U.S. foreign policy. What is at stake is considerable by any measure. Pakistan is the world's second-most-populous Muslim-majority country, with nearly 170 million people. It shares borders with Afghanistan, where U.S. and allied forces are struggling to promote stability amid a continuing insurgency, and India, with which it has fought a series of conflicts. Pakistan's nuclear arsenal and history of abetting proliferation put it in a position to dilute global efforts to stem the spread of nuclear materials and weapons. And it is host to local extremist groups, the Taliban, and global terrorist organizations, most notably al-Qaeda.

The relationship between the United States and Pakistan has long been characterized by cooperation and recrimination alike. Pakistan is a strategic friend of the United States, but one that often appears unable or unwilling to address a number of vexing security concerns. Political disarray has further hampered Islamabad's capacity for strong and united action. The result in Washington is often frustration mixed with uncertainty about what to do about it.

Few dimensions of dealing with Pakistan are the source of as much frustration as the tribal areas bordering Afghanistan, the subject of this Council Special Report commissioned by the Center for Preventive Action. Daniel Markey analyzes the unique challenges of this region, which has long been largely outside Pakistani government control. He argues that the United States must work with Islamabad to confront security threats and improve governance and economic opportunity in the Federally Administered Tribal Areas (FATA), something that could reduce militancy. The report lays out a cooperative, incentives-based strategy for the United States that would aim to increase the capacity of the Pakistani government and its security institutions, foster political and economic reform, and build confidence in the bilateral relationship. At the same time, the report outlines alternatives to be considered should this positive approach fail to advance U.S. interests. These alternatives, be they coercive sanctions to induce Pakistan to act or unilateral U.S. action against security threats, could bring some short-term progress in dealing with significant threats— but at the cost of bringing about a more hostile Pakistan that would cease to be a partner of any sort.

There is no way to escape either the difficulties or the dilemmas. *Securing Pakistan's Tribal Belt* is a thorough and knowledgeable examination of a critical set of issues involving Pakistan, the United States, and much more. The report offers detailed and wide-ranging recommendations for a country and a region that has long challenged U.S. leaders and that is sure to be a priority of the next U.S. administration as well.

Richard N. Haass
President
Council on Foreign Relations
July 2008

Acknowledgments

I am grateful to the Center for Preventive Action (CPA) at the Council on Foreign Relations (CFR) for sponsoring this report. This sponsorship included a timely and very helpful research trip to Pakistan. Thanks to CPA Director Paul B. Stares for taking on the project and offering supportive and insightful advice along the way. Thanks also to Jamie Ekern for her quick and meticulous editing and organizational efforts.

I am especially indebted to Daniel Simons, whose thoughtful and tireless research assistance has been invaluable at each and every stage of this project.

CFR President Richard N. Haass and Director of Studies Gary Samore each provided helpful comments on drafts. Thanks go to Patricia Dorff and Lia Norton in Publications and to Lisa Shields and Aerica Kennedy in Communications for their contributions. Several CFR interns have served as able researchers, including Katherine Hall, Lena Hull, Yariv Pierce, and Will Nomikos.

A number of individuals have provided valuable feedback at various points in the research and drafting of this report, including Khalid Aziz, Amanda Catanzano, Amy B. Frumin, K. Alan Kronstadt, Shuja Nawaz, Richard Sokolsky, Robert M. Traister, and Tariq Zaheen. This report also benefited from a great number of interviews with Pakistani and American analysts and government officials who prefer to go unnamed.

Members of an advisory committee generously provided time and assistance, some in person and others by way of extensive email exchanges. This committee included Stanley S. Arkin, Jonah Blank, Steve Coll, James F. Dobbins, Frederic Grare, Paul E. Greenwood,

Robert L. Grenier, Seth G. Jones, David J. Katz, Paul Matulic, John E. McLaughlin, Polly Nayak, Robert B. Oakley, Michelle S. Parker, Jonathan L. Sperling, Ashley J. Tellis, and Joshua T. White.

This publication was made possible by a grant from the Carnegie Corporation of New York. The statements made and views expressed herein are solely my own.

Daniel Markey

Maps

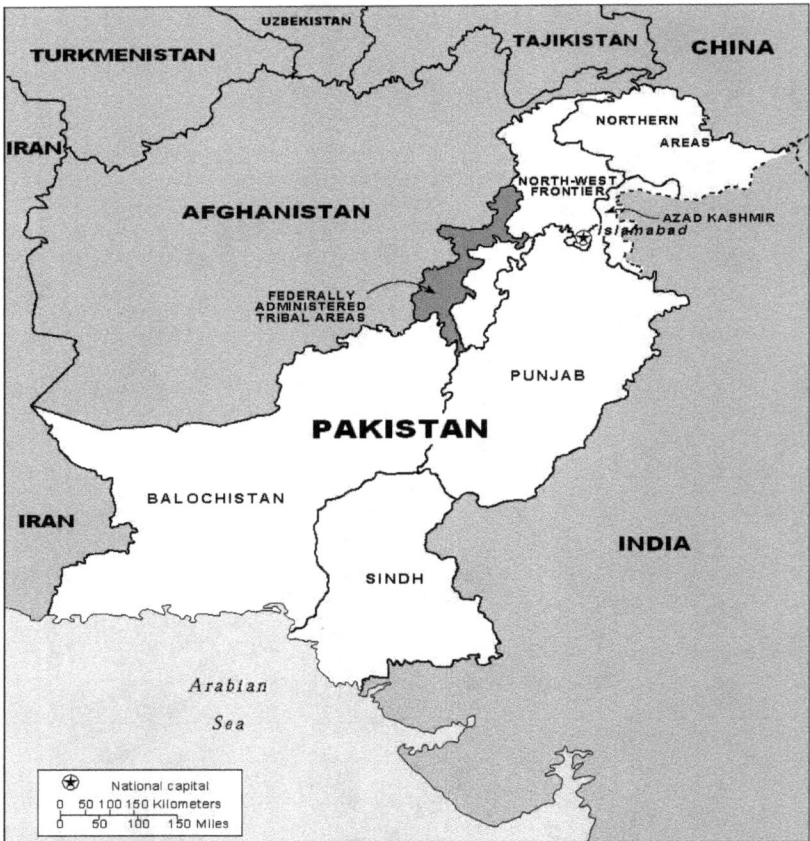

Source: Modified from http://lcweb2.loc.gov/frd/cs/pakistan/pk00_07a.pdf.

Pakistan and the Surrounding Region

Source: Modified from http://commons.wikimedia.org/wiki/Image:NWFP_and_FATA.jpg.

Pakistan's Tribal Belt

Acronyms

CENTCOM	United States Central Command
DCG	Defense Consultative Group
FATA	Federally Administered Tribal Areas
FC	Frontier Corps
FCR	Frontier Crimes Regulation
ISAF	International Security Assistance Force
ISI	Inter-Services Intelligence
JI	Jamaat-e-Islami
JUI-F	Jamiat Ulema-e-Islam (Fazlur Rehman faction)
LI	Lashkar-e-Islam
NATO	North Atlantic Treaty Organization
NSC	National Security Council
NWFP	North-West Frontier Province
ODRP	Office of Defense Representative, Pakistan
OTI	Office of Transition Initiatives
PATA	Provincially Administered Tribal Areas
ROZ	Reconstruction Opportunity Zone
TNSM	Tehreek-e-Nafaz-e-Shariat-e-Mohammadi
TTP	Tehrik-i-Taliban Pakistan
UAE	United Arab Emirates
USAID	United States Agency for International Development

Council Special Report

Introduction

Today, few places on earth are as important to U.S. national security as the tribal belt along Pakistan's border with Afghanistan. The region serves as a safe haven for a core group of nationally and internationally networked terrorists, a training and recruiting ground for Afghan Taliban, and, increasingly, a hotbed of indigenous militancy that threatens the stability of Pakistan's own state and society. Should another 9/11-type attack take place in the United States, it will likely have its origins in this region. As long as Pakistan's tribal areas are in turmoil, the mission of building a new, democratic, and stable Afghanistan cannot succeed.

Nearly seven years after 9/11, neither the United States nor Pakistan has fully come to terms with the enormity of the challenge in the tribal belt. Washington has failed to convince Pakistanis that the United States has positive intentions in the region and is committed to staying the course long enough to implement lasting, constructive change. Pakistan, for its part, has demonstrated a disturbing lack of capacity and, all too often, an apparent lack of will to tackle head-on the security, political, or developmental deficits that have produced an explosion of terrorism and extremism within its borders and beyond. Islamabad's conflicted views and priorities with respect to this fight have deep roots; for much of its history, the Pakistani state has employed militants as tools to project power and influence throughout the region.[1]

In order to begin making progress in the tribal areas, the United States must build strong working relationships with Pakistani leaders and institutions, both military and civilian. The alternatives, ranging from reluctant, piecemeal cooperation to an outright rupture in bilateral relations, are bound to be far more costly and counterproductive to American interests over the long run. And despite the inevitable frustrations that will plague the U.S.-Pakistan partnership, it cannot be founded on coercive threats of U.S. sanctions or unilateral military activity. Such coercion is profoundly counterproductive because it empowers those in Pakistan who already suspect U.S. ill intentions and it undermines Washington's real and potential allies in the Pakistani political system.

Rather than threats, Washington should employ a strategy of enhanced cooperation and structured inducements, in which the United States designs its assistance to bring U.S. and Pakistani officials closer together and provides Pakistan with the specific tools required to confront the threats posed by militancy, terrorism, and extremism.

In his first six months in office, the new U.S. president should articulate a formal, comprehensive vision for U.S. policy in the tribal areas, one that prepares both Americans and Pakistanis for a cooperative effort that extends to other facets of the bilateral relationship and will—even if successful—far outlast the next administration. The U.S. government should place Pakistan/ Afghanistan second only to Iraq in its prioritization of immediate national security issues, and should move quickly to reassess assistance programming and to invest in U.S. personnel and institutions required for a long-term commitment to the region.

This report aims to characterize the nature of the challenges in Pakistan's tribal areas, formulate strategies for addressing these challenges, and distill these strategies into realistic policy proposals worthy of consideration by the incoming administration. It focuses mainly on U.S. policy, but recognizes that Washington's choices must always be contingent upon Pakistan's own course of action. The scope of this report is thus more constrained than exhaustive, and its recommendations for U.S. assistance programming are intended to provide strategic guidelines rather than narrow prescriptions.

Background and Context

THE LAND AND PEOPLE OF PAKISTAN'S TRIBAL BELT

Harsh geography, poor education, and scarce infrastructure have tended to drive a wedge between Pakistan's tribal belt and the rest of the nation.[2] With an estimated population of 3.5 million—out of a total Pakistani population of nearly 170 million—the Federally Administered Tribal Areas (FATA), at approximately 10,500 square miles, are roughly the same size as the state of Maryland and share nearly three hundred miles of border with Afghanistan. The entire Pakistani-Afghan border runs 1,640 miles of difficult, widely differentiated terrain, from the southern deserts of Balochistan to the northern mountain peaks of the North-West Frontier Province (NWFP).

The FATA is the poorest, least developed part of Pakistan. Literacy is only 17 percent, compared to the national average of 40 percent; among women it is 3 percent, compared to the national average of 32 percent. Per capita income is roughly $250—half the national average of $500. Nearly 66 percent of households live beneath the poverty line. Only ten thousand workers now find employment in the FATA's industrial sector. The FATA's forbidding terrain further serves to isolate tribal communities from markets, health and education services, and many outside influences.

Pashtun tribes straddle the Pakistani-Afghan border, and the vast majority of Pashtuns live outside the FATA. This ethnic group numbers approximately forty million, and subdivides into units of varying size, primarily based on kinship ties. Analytically, Pashtuns have been characterized as either hill or lowland tribes, with the latter typically more integrated into national (either Pakistani or Afghan) politics and economics. The hill tribes are often depicted as being driven by a fierce concern with personal and group honor, or nang.

Invaders have crisscrossed the tribal areas for hundreds of years, and the Pashtun tribes have gained a celebrated reputation for their independence and martial spirit. Aside from their common use of the Pashto language (and related dialects), Pashtuns also affirm their unity through a code of conduct, or Pashtunwali, that describes a constellation of ideal-type virtues and values intended to guide them in all situations. Much of the literature on Pashtuns depicts these virtues as relating to concepts of hospitality, granting of pardons, and redress of wrongs, but the specifics are open to interpretation. In addition, Pashtuns have developed the jirga process—a dispute resolution mechanism that relies upon a consensus decision by adult male members of the community rather than on formalized criminal statutes applied by an impartial judge.

The vast majority of Pashtuns are Sunni Muslims. Over history, sharply divided and independent Pashtun clans have unified periodically under the banner of charismatic religious leaders, typically in response to external pressures. This aspect of Pashtun identity has gained special prominence in recent decades, but with a new twist. During Afghanistan's anti-Soviet jihad of the 1980s, local religious leaders, or mullahs, translated an influx of financial support into a massive expansion of extremist-minded seminaries, or madrassas, which trained a generation of students in Islamist militancy. In the post-9/11 period, a younger, even more radical generation has often prevailed over—and in some cases eliminated—tribal elders, thereby upsetting traditional political and social structures.

GOVERNING INSTITUTIONS

Pakistan's tribal belt falls under four territorially defined mechanisms of governance. The first is the FATA. There are seven tribal agencies

(Khyber, Kurram, North and South Waziristan, Mohmand, Bajaur, Orakzai) and six Frontier Regions (Peshawar, Tank, Bannu, Kohat, Lakki, Dera Ismail Khan) in the FATA. By virtue of a special, semiautonomous status negotiated at Pakistan's independence and reaffirmed in subsequent national constitutions, the president of Pakistan directly administers the FATA through the governor of NWFP and his appointed political agents. Although the FATA has elected representatives to Pakistan's National Assembly since the mid-1990s, national legislation does not apply to the FATA. Also, Pakistan's political parties are legally barred from contesting seats there (i.e., all elected representatives are technically unaffiliated).

The FATA is not subject to rulings by national or provincial courts. Instead, it falls under the Frontier Crimes Regulation (FCR), a legal system adopted by Pakistan at independence and rooted in British colonial practice and traditional tribal jirgas. Under the FCR, disputes between tribes and the Pakistani state are managed through the interaction of political agents and tribal representatives, or maliks. Given the egalitarian character of Pashtun society, maliks are best understood as primus inter pares, rather than strong figures of authority. In this respect, Pashtun tribes are quite different from their counterparts in Balochistan, where tribal leaders (sardars) can command far greater hierarchical authority.[3] The political agent is empowered to coerce tribesmen through threats and bribes. His coercive power includes collective punishment of a tribe for the actions of individual members and his rulings are not subject to judicial review or appeal. The political agent's executive authority is backed by a local constabulary force (levies and khassadars), and, under more extreme circumstances, by the Frontier Corps (FC) and Pakistani army. All purely internal administrative and policing functions are managed by the tribes themselves.

The FATA's system of governance is correctly criticized for its lack of democratic accountability and failure to observe basic standards of human rights. Political parties have long advocated opening the region to normal party competition by extending the national Political Parties Act. In his inaugural address, Prime Minister Yousaf Raza Gillani proposed a more drastic transformation: repeal of the FCR. Despite periodic calls for reform, those empowered by the status quo—including some tribal elders, bureaucrats, and the military-dominated government in Islamabad—have to this point successfully resisted change.[4] A recent survey of FATA residents suggests that while there is strong support for amending the FCR, there is little consensus on what should replace it.[5] Since tribesmen now enjoy substantial autonomy in their own affairs as well as a variety of government stipends and privileges (including free, if inconsistent, access to electricity), and since tribal territory is collectively owned, the wholesale or rapid integration of the FATA into the rest of Pakistan raises complicated political and legal hurdles, and would be sure to spark protest.

The second type of governing mechanism is the Provincially Administered Tribal Areas (PATA), made up of seven of the twenty-four districts of the NWFP and five territories within Balochistan. A number of these districts were princely states incorporated into Pakistan as of the early 1970s and now administered by provincial authorities. The PATA transition has proven to be a rocky one. Weak governance in parts of the PATA, especially in the judicial and law enforcement spheres, has raised calls for the implementation of sharia, or Islamic law, as an alternative to corruption and inefficiency. Observers of tribal politics note that there is no single popular understanding of what "sharia law" should mean, suggesting that it may be far more popular in the abstract hypothetical than in formal implementation, especially if implementation resembles the harsh rule of the Taliban in Afghanistan. Leaders of the Tehreek-e-Nafaz-e-Shariat-e-Mohammadi (TNSM), an anti-state militant organization that temporarily took over the Swat Valley in 2007, have proven especially skillful at harnessing the appeal of sharia to win popular support. The failure to integrate the PATA seamlessly into the North-West Frontier Province suggests some important pitfalls to avoid when considering institutional reforms in the FATA.[6]

The last two governing mechanisms of the tribal areas are the provincial governments of Balochistan and NWFP, where national and provincial laws apply in the same way as in Pakistan's other two provinces, Punjab and Sindh. But shared laws and assemblies have not translated readily into shared interests. In particular, the historically dominant role played by Punjab has long fueled resentment in Pakistan's smaller provinces. Recently, interprovincial disputes have raged over the distribution of revenues from natural resources (gas from Balochistan, water and hydropower from NWFP) and the construction of large dams for electricity and irrigation. To be sure, political and ethnic cleavages run deep in Pakistan and are not limited to territorial boundaries. Violent conflicts between Pashtuns and other groups have raged outside the tribal areas, most notably in Karachi, which is both Pakistan's most important financial center and home to more ethnic Pashtuns than any other city in the world.

SECURITY FORCES

The multiple layers of governing institutions in the tribal areas are matched by a variety of security forces.

Within the FATA, levies and khassadars serve under the authority of the political agent. These forces numbered over 23,000 in 2005–2006. They are trained to do light policing, guard government facilities, and secure public figures. In NWFP and Balochistan, provincial police report through the civil service hierarchy, but each force is also headed by an inspector general who is directly accountable to the Interior Ministry in Islamabad. As of 2007, there were 48,000 police serving in NWFP and 46,022 in Balochistan. Pakistan's police can be called into duty by the federal government for national security missions, but they are trained and equipped only to handle standard criminal investigations.

The Frontier Constabulary is an additional policing organization in the tribal belt, recruited from the settled districts outside the FATA and commanded by officers from the provincial police force. Originally intended to secure the territories just outside the FATA from smuggling and crime, the Frontier Constabulary also performs various light operations throughout NWFP and other parts of Pakistan.

The Frontier Corps is the primary paramilitary force in the tribal areas. For most of its history, the FC has served as a border control and countersmuggling force, on call for law enforcement operations in FATA and the provinces. It is organized under two commands—NWFP and Balochistan—with separate headquarters in Peshawar and Quetta, respectively. In total, the FC consists of roughly eighty thousand troops. Each command is headed by a major general in the Pakistani army, and regular army officers staff senior FC positions on two- to three-year tours.

Because the troops of the FC are recruited and trained locally and administered by Pakistan's Interior Ministry, the organization is fundamentally distinct from the regular army. Historically, this separation has been reflected through inattention to the quality of FC training and equipment. This negligence was manageable as long as the FC faced lesser threats, but in recent years its units have been tasked to confront well-outfitted and battle-hardened militants. Unsurprisingly, in most instances the FC fared poorly, losing over three hundred troops since 2001 and regularly abandoning posts. In addition to weak capacity, critics have raised questions about the allegiances of the FC's Pashtun rank-and-file found in the North-West Frontier Province, particularly when it comes to fighting Taliban and other Pashtun militants.

Throughout Pakistan's history, the army has served as the nation's preeminent security institution. It has also regularly dominated politics in Islamabad. Indeed, the persistent imbalance in Pakistan's civil-military relationship is the defining feature of the national political dynamic. The army's XI Corps, responsible for NWFP and the Afghan border, is headquartered in Peshawar. It consists of two divisions, the 7th and 9th. In order to deal with the upsurge in violence in the tribal areas, the 14th division (normally based in Punjab) has recently reinforced XI Corps operations.

Since 9/11, Pakistan's army has played a historically unprecedented role in the tribal areas, where the government under Pervez Musharraf pursued discordant strategies, rotating between heavy military occupation and political negotiation. In June 2002, the army deployed a division into Khyber and Kurram agencies to block al-Qaeda and other terrorists from escaping U.S. attacks in Afghanistan. By 2004, however, it was clear that terrorists had gained a significant foothold in the FATA, especially in North Waziristan and South Waziristan, so the Pakistani army began a series of major search-and-destroy missions. These operations were deeply unpopular and met with widespread resistance, in part because they constituted the army's first major incursions into the FATA since Pakistan's independence. This "invasion" was seen as a violation of the promise by Pakistan's founding father, Mohammad Ali Jinnah, not to send troops into the FATA for any operation and instead to resolve disputes through negotiations and jirgas.

Accepting the army's poor capacity to manage a lengthy occupation of the Waziristans, and sensitive to the prospect of further alienating tribal populations, Musharraf's regime undertook a series of controversial settlements with militants and local leaders. These included, notably, the South Waziristan accords of April 2004 and February 2005 as well as the North Waziristan accord of September 2006. On paper, these accords obligated locals to cease their anti-state activities. Early on, however, it became clear that the settlements suffered from weak enforcement, permitting the continued sanctuary of foreign terrorists and cross-border infiltration of militants into Afghanistan. The United States alleged cross-border infiltration increased 300 percent after the 2006 North Waziristan agreement went into effect.

The politically tumultuous events of 2007 also brought the Pakistani army into action in settled parts of the country. In July, army commandos stormed the Lal Masjid, or Red Mosque, in Islamabad to crush an anti-state uprising, sparking terrorist attacks against government facilities as well as innocent civilians. Over seven hundred Pakistanis have died in suicide bombings in the year since July 2007. The army also undertook major combat operations post-November 3 (when Musharraf declared a state of emergency) to break TNSM's hold over the Swat Valley.

The Pakistani army was not built to conduct counterinsurgency or counterterror missions. Post-9/11 operations against Pakistani nationals—whether in the FATA, NWFP, or elsewhere—have been broadly unpopular and characterized as "Washington's war." By the end of 2007, rising domestic antipathy toward Musharraf's military-led government precipitated a drop in the normally high esteem accorded to army officers and enlisted men. By many anecdotal accounts, morale in the ranks has plummeted, with predictably disastrous implications for combat effectiveness.

In addition to police, paramilitary, and army forces, Pakistan's intelligence services are widely reported to play an active part in the tribal areas. In the 1980s, the Inter-Services Intelligence (ISI) worked in the tribal areas as the primary conduit of assistance from the United States and Saudi Arabia to the Afghan mujahadeen. ISI support for different jihadi groups, including the Taliban, continued throughout the 1990s.

The post-9/11 relationship between ISI and different militant operations is the subject of intense debate. Since most ISI officers are seconded from the regular Pakistani army, its characterization as a "rogue" intelligence agency is ill founded. But ISI remains the Pakistani government's primary covert arm, and Pakistan's long-standing interest in projecting influence into Afghanistan and India may still color ISI interactions with a variety of militant organizations.

MUSHARRAF'S "COMPREHENSIVE APPROACH" AND POST-ELECTION DEAL-MAKING

From 2006 to 2007, the Musharraf government began to implement a "comprehensive approach" in the FATA that envisioned the use of limited security operations in combination with political overtures and development assistance. The strategy was intended to combat the underlying causes of militancy by enhancing economic opportunities and improving the legitimacy of state institutions. Islamabad's development plan was centered on a nine-year, $2 billion commitment to programming by Pakistan and other donors.[7]

But extreme political turbulence through most of 2007 and into 2008 has distracted Islamabad's attention from the tribal areas. An unanticipated upsurge of popular anti-regime protests was first energized by a grassroots campaign against President Musharraf's attempted removal of Chief Justice Iftikhar Mohammad Chaudhry in spring 2007. In a whirlwind that grabbed global headlines throughout the summer and fall, exiled opposition politicians Benazir Bhutto and Nawaz Sharif returned to campaign for national elections; Musharraf declared a state of emergency to remove the uncooperative Supreme Court justices, ratify his election to the presidency, and pave the way for his resignation from the army; and during the campaigning process for parliamentary elections Bhutto was assassinated by a suicide bomber on December 27, 2007. In early 2008, Bhutto's husband, Asif Zardari, assumed control over the Pakistan Peoples Party, which emerged from elections as the head of a governing coalition that included Nawaz Sharif's faction of the Pakistan Muslim League.

As of summer 2008, the political dynamic in Islamabad remains extremely fluid. Facing threats of impeachment, Musharraf resigned from office on August 18, exactly six months after national elections. Musharraf's successor as chief of army staff, General Ashfaq Parvez Kiyani, has studiously steered clear of political intrigue. Zardari and Sharif have alternated between cooperation and rivalry, and continue to engage in a marathon series of political negotiations on everything from the restoration of the supreme court to power sharing arrangements in the federal cabinet.

Uncertainty in Islamabad has so far yielded a fragmented approach to the tribal areas. The army appears to be pursuing a strategy conceived prior to elections, which—aside from punitive operations in South Waziristan—has tended to place the Frontier Corps on the front lines in managing militant threats. Pakistan's new civilian leaders have not taken an especially firm hand with the army, exercising only loose command or oversight. By some accounts, ISI has assumed the lead on negotiations with tribal groups, most notably the Mehsuds of South Waziristan.[8] On a parallel track, the newly elected provincial leaders in Peshawar have forged deals with TNSM militants in a localized bid to end violence in the Swat Valley.

To improve coordination across the branches of the government, the prime minister's secretariat released a statement on June 25, 2008, establishing principles for action in the tribal areas—including the FATA and NWFP—and designating jurisdictions and responsibilities to the governor, provincial ministers, and army.[9] The statement essentially reaffirmed Islamabad's commitment to the "comprehensive approach," identifying the continued need for a "multi-pronged strategy" that includes political, military, and economic components.

PAKISTAN-AFGHANISTAN RELATIONS

Since 1947, Pakistan-Afghanistan relations have nearly always been rocky. Pakistan's leadership has tended to perceive the politics of Pashtun ethnicity, which transcends national borders, as a threat to national sovereignty. This insecurity is fueled by Kabul's persistent dispute over the demarcation of Pakistan's western border, known as the Durand Line. Territorial disputes—and armed skirmishes—have been a regular feature of the bilateral relationship. Pakistani proposals to fence or mine the border are understood by Afghans as thinly disguised efforts to ratify an unacceptable territorial status quo. Pakistan has also vigorously pursued repatriation of Afghan refugees to their homeland, with over 3.2 million Afghans returning home since 2002, and the remainder—at least two million—set to be expelled by 2009.

The flow of money, arms, and people between Afghanistan and Pakistan's tribal areas has profoundly influenced political dynamics in the FATA. Human and material cross-border movement has connected smugglers, militants, and the narcotics trade. Millions of Afghan refugees and their sprawling city-like camps have, over decades, become a near-permanent presence in Pakistan, one that poses tremendous political, social, and economic challenges.

In recent decades, Pakistan's influence in Afghan politics and warfare has represented a more significant cause of friction. Above all, by continuing to offer a permissive environment for Afghan Taliban operations, Pakistan represents an existential threat to President Karzai's government in Kabul.

From Islamabad's perspective, Afghanistan holds strategic value in regional contests against Iran and India. This perspective compels Pakistan to seek a friendly regime in Kabul. Most notably, in the mid-1990s, it led Benazir Bhutto's government to support the creation and rise to power of the Taliban. Since 2002, Islamabad has suspiciously eyed Indian activities in Afghanistan, perceived as attempts to encircle Pakistan. Pakistan's most frequent complaints center on India's consulates in Jalalabad and Kandahar, but India's wide-ranging construction, training, and assistance programs are all seen as blatant efforts to forge an anti-Pakistan alliance.

Efforts to improve relations between the governments of Hamid Karzai and Pervez Musharraf tended to be more symbolic than tangible. The United States and Turkey have each hosted Pakistani-Afghan summits in a bid to soothe contentious interactions at the senior-most levels. In August 2007, Karzai and Musharraf met at a joint "peace jirga" in Kabul and pledged to convene smaller working groups in the future.

On the military side, Tripartite Commission meetings of commanding officers from Pakistan, Afghanistan, and the United States/North Atlantic Treaty Organization (NATO) have at times provided a vital channel for strategic policy coordination. U.S. officials are hopeful that the establishment of a Joint Intelligence Operations Center in Kabul—staffed by officers from NATO, Pakistan, and Afghanistan—as well as the six Border Coordination Centers planned for construction on both sides of the border will facilitate the sharing of tactical intelligence and gradually build greater trust.

MAPPING THE THREATS IN PAKISTAN'S TRIBAL AREAS

Within Pakistan's tribal areas are at least four overlapping but analytically discernable security threats: global terrorists; Afghan Taliban; Pakistani Taliban; and a plethora of tribal militias, extremist networks, and sectarian groups.

The July 2007 U.S. National Intelligence Estimate on "The Terrorist Threat to the U.S. Homeland" and subsequent statements by top officials reflect a consensus view that al-Qaeda's leadership remains ensconced in the Pakistani-Afghan border region, from where it continues to plan, fund, and inspire attacks.[10] That al-Qaeda leadership is accompanied by between 150 and 500 hard-core fighters. In addition, other foreign terrorist organizations affiliated with al-Qaeda and previously based in Afghanistan, especially Uzbeks, now operate from the FATA. Estimates of Uzbek fighters in Waziristan run between one thousand and two thousand.

The Afghan Taliban, forced from power in 2002, has managed to regroup and direct operations from Pakistan's side of the border. The former leadership—including Mullah Omar—is said to be based in Quetta, the provincial capital of Balochistan. A major Taliban-affiliated network, now led by Sirajuddin Haqqani, is based in North Waziristan, from where it has successfully launched attacks on U.S., Afghan, and NATO forces in Afghanistan.

The links between the Afghan Taliban and al-Qaeda are ideological, personal, and operational, but to some degree the groups diverge in prioritization of goals and ethnic composition. The Afghan Taliban are a Pashtun movement primarily concerned with the reconquest and domination of Afghanistan and only secondarily with the Arab-led al-Qaeda's grander schemes of global jihad. However, over the past six years it appears that the Taliban have become more decentralized operationally, more sophisticated tactically, and more influenced ideologically by foreign Arab fighters.

Estimates of total Afghan Taliban strength run to ten thousand, with 20 percent to 30 percent full-time fighters and 1 percent to 3 percent foreign (non-Pashtun).[11] In Pakistan, Taliban recruits are drawn from Afghan refugee camps and the network of extremist madrassas in the tribal areas. Taliban foot soldiers tend to be uneducated, poor Pashtuns with few other employment prospects.

The Pakistani Taliban is a loosely defined mix of tribal militant groups, many of whom united under the banner of the Tehrik-i-Taliban Pakistan (TTP) in December 2007.[12] The TTP includes representatives from throughout the FATA and NWFP. It is nominally directed by the now infamous Baitullah Mehsud, alleged mastermind of the Benazir Bhutto assassination. Meshud has sworn allegiance to Afghan Taliban leader Mullah Omar, but his public pronouncements have also assumed the rhetoric of an al-Qaeda-like global jihad, including threats against the White House, New York, and London.

Then again, it might be more appropriate to understand the Pakistani Taliban as focused on concerns closer to home, such as the implementation of sharia and waging a "defensive jihad" against the Pakistani army occupation of tribal territories. Indeed, the TTP's true motivations—whether defensive or offensive; local, regional, or global—are an important and unanswered question. It is not clear, for instance, whether the Pakistani Taliban might be cleaved from the Afghan Taliban and/or al-Qaeda in a bid to satisfy localized demands.

Estimates of TTP strength run to over twenty thousand tribesmen, and Mehsud is said to command at least five thousand fighters. He is likely responsible for a rash of suicide bombings throughout Pakistan over the past year. A small contingent of his forces also made headlines when they managed to take hostage over 250 Pakistani soldiers in August 2007. By all appearances, the Pakistani Taliban now represents the greatest threat to security within Pakistan.

Significant militant groups other than the TTP include the TNSM in Bajaur Agency, Swat District, and neighboring areas of the NWFP, founded by the pro-Taliban Sufi Mohammad and more recently commanded by his son-in-law, the popular and charismatic "Radio Mullah" Fazlullah. In South Waziristan, a tribal militia under the command of Maulvi Nazir apparently received Pakistani government support in factional fighting against Uzbek militants over the past year.

And in Khyber Agency, another radio mullah, Mangal Bagh Afridi, leads Lashkar-e-Islam (LI), a militant group that has resisted association with the TTP, is active all the way to the outskirts of Peshawar, and desires Taliban-style government.

Besides the Afghan Taliban, militants in Balochistan include those with more localized grievances against Islamabad that are related, in part, to the inequitable distribution of provincial and national resources.[13] In recent years, the violence of the Baloch insurgency has imposed significant costs on the Pakistani army and security forces, distracted the political leadership in Islamabad, and contributed to national instability.

In addition, nationwide Islamist political parties like Jamaat-e-Islami (JI) and Jamiat Ulema-e-Islam (Fazlur Rehman's faction, or the JUI-F) also appear to have connections to al-Qaeda and other militant operations in the tribal areas. These ties are based on personal relationships, ideological affinity, or tactical unity of interest. Historically, the large network of JUI-F–organized Deobandi madrassas churned out thousands of indoctrinated foot soldiers, sent to fight first for the Afghan mujahadeen, and then the Taliban.[14]In addition, there is evidence to suggest that Pakistani militant groups such as Jaish-e-Mohammed and Lashkar-e-Taiba have, in recent years, become more connected to global terror plots in addition to retaining their traditional focus on operations in Kashmir. These organizations were long nurtured by the Pakistani security apparatus, and their current relationship to the Pakistani establishment is difficult to discern with certainty. Regardless, while Pakistan's terror problem may begin in the tribal areas, militant networks are now entrenched throughout the country.

U.S. POLICY IN THE TRIBAL AREAS

Washington's early post-9/11 involvement in Pakistan's tribal areas tended to be indirect, focusing on a liaison relationship with (and financial assistance to) Pakistan's government and security forces. This relationship was based on President Musharraf's agreement to support U.S. operations against al-Qaeda and the remnants of the Afghan Taliban regime in return for Washington's pledge to respect Pakistan's sovereignty. Pakistan remains an essential—perhaps even irreplaceable—link in the massive logistics chain for U.S. and NATO forces operating in Afghanistan. As of October 2007, approximately 40 percent of fuel (roughly equal to 120,000 gallons per day) and 84 percent of all containerized cargo for delivery to coalition forces operating in Afghanistan passed through Pakistan.[15]

Judging from publicly available accounts, most recent U.S. and NATO missions have been limited to Afghan soil, with three exceptions: U.S. investigations to locate and arrest senior al-Qaeda operatives in Pakistan; cases of hot pursuit in which U.S. forces fired upon or briefly chased militants into Pakistan; and the use of U.S. Predator drones to track and strike al-Qaeda and Taliban leadership based in the FATA.[16] The administration of George W. Bush has elected not to risk a U.S. ground presence in Pakistan out of concern for the costs it might impose on U.S.-Pakistan relations or on Pakistan's political stability, given the expected popular backlash in the tribal areas and beyond.

The vast majority of U.S. post-9/11 assistance to Pakistan has gone to the military. According to a recent Government Accountability Office study, from October 2001 through June 2007, the United States reimbursed Pakistan over $5.5 billion for operations undertaken in support of U.S. and International Security Assistance Force (ISAF)/NATO efforts in Afghanistan. In addition, Washington has provided $1.52 billion since 2002 as part of a five-year, $3 billion presidential assistance package.[17] Not until FY2008 were these funds congressionally circumscribed for use only in "counterterrorism and law enforcement activities directed against al-Qaeda and the Taliban and associated terrorist groups." The Pakistani military relies on the United States for roughly a quarter of its $4 billion budget.

Nonmilitary assistance over the same time frame has totaled roughly $3.1 billion. The combined security and economic aid from 2002 to 2008 was $10.9 billion, the vast majority of which was (until

2008) provided as direct budget support to the Pakistani government.[18] U.S. civilian assistance programming has focused on Pakistan's education and health sectors. Additional U.S. aid was provided in the aftermath of the October 2005 earthquake, including extensive military involvement in humanitarian logistics.

Until quite recently, U.S. assistance—both military and civilian—lacked a specific focus on the tribal areas. This changed in response to President Musharraf's March 2006 request for support to advance his new "comprehensive approach" in the FATA. The Bush administration has pledged $750 million over five years in FATA-specific development assistance, complemented by significant new funds for enhancing Pakistan's capacity for counterinsurgency, counterterrorism, and border control.

On the civilian side, the U.S. Agency for International Development (USAID)'s Pakistan mission and the Office of Transition Initiatives (OTI) are programming and contracting most of the $750 million FATA package. By far the largest single piece ($300 million through 2012) will go to a "Livelihoods Development Program," including cash-for-work, infrastructure, and vocational training programs intended to offer alternatives for young tribesmen who otherwise have few choices but gun toting.

Poor security and lack of access to the FATA pose significant challenges to U.S. assistance programming. USAID officials, their implementing partners, and Pakistani employees are now severely constrained in their movements, limiting implementation and oversight, particularly in those areas most ravaged by insurgency. But despite protests from Pakistani officials, nearly all U.S. funds will be channeled through private contractors, raising questions about overhead costs. USAID has allocated $88 million to support local government capacity and outreach through 2009, which may signal a greater likelihood of direct budget support (rather than contractor-based programming) in the future.

Other development efforts include the Bush administration's plan for Reconstruction Opportunity Zones (ROZs), which would offer duty-free access to the U.S. market for certain types of goods produced in factories in or near Pakistan's tribal areas. ROZs require congressional legislation and might serve as one part of a wider effort to spur private investment.[19] Other states, including the United Kingdom and Japan, are also making major contributions to development efforts in Pakistan.[20] Relatively fewer U.S. assistance programs target the tribal areas outside the FATA. U.S. activity in Balochistan is particularly limited.

Following a U.S. Central Command (CENTCOM) assessment, the Pentagon has formulated a FATA Security Development Plan devoted to improving the FC, with a price tag running to roughly $400 million over the next several years. An initial 2007 injection of $150 million was devoted to the establishment of two FC training facilities near Quetta and Peshawar, six Border Coordination Centers, four sector headquarters, two intelligence bases, and the gradual addition of eight additional FC wings (700 to 800 troops each) and two new intelligence battalions. A limited number of U.S. trainers will train Pakistani trainers in counterinsurgency tactics, and the Pentagon is providing the FC with body armor, vehicles, radios, and surveillance equipment.

A Comprehensive Strategy

FACING UP TO THE IMMENSITY OF THE CHALLENGE

The years since 9/11 have validated the fact that the pacification of Pakistan's tribal belt represents a necessary (if insufficient) condition for eliminating al-Qaeda, enabling reconstruction in Afghanistan, and maintaining domestic stability in Pakistan. But the immense scale and complexity of this challenge is currently underappreciated in both Washington and Islamabad.

The Pakistani government lacks the political, military, or bureaucratic capacity to fix the tribal areas on its own. Islamabad's civilian political leaders have little recent experience in dealing with a development and security initiative of this scale; at present, they appear far more concerned with skirmishing over power than developing an effective policy for the tribal areas. The pathological imbalance between civilian and military power at the national level continues to hinder stable, efficient governance, and, particularly over the past eighteen months, has provided a formula mainly for lurching from crisis to crisis.

Pakistan's army has not come to terms with the need to fundamentally retool itself for a new counterinsurgency mission, one far different from its historical fixation on war with India. The FC and other policing forces throughout the tribal areas are ill prepared to pick up the army's slack, at least in the immediate term. Local judicial and administrative institutions, such as the political agents in the FATA and the lower courts of the NWFP, are widely perceived as corrupt and inefficient, if not outright illegitimate. And Pakistan's long history of involvement in Afghanistan offers no insulation from the flare of regional tensions.

Moreover, because of a yawning trust deficit between Pakistan and the United States, Washington cannot even be sure that Islamabad shares its interests, or at least its priorities, in the tribal areas. In particular, Pakistan appears far more concerned about immediate threats to internal security than to militancy in Afghanistan or terrorism in the United States and Western Europe. Most Pakistanis tend to believe that U.S. intervention in Afghanistan was more a cause of regional instability than a response to it. Anti-Americanism is widespread and profound. In a national May/June 2008 poll, only 16.9 percent of Pakistanis had a very or somewhat favorable view of the United States, the lowest popularity rating of all the countries surveyed and less than half that of India.[21]

This lack of unambiguous Pakistani support for the U.S. agenda and the potential for popular Pakistani backlash against visible American intervention handcuff Washington's policy options. Still, Pakistan remains a fragile, internally divided state more than a rogue or enemy. Washington should not yet give in to the frustrations of dealing with its conflicted ally and seek to go it alone; given the enormous repercussions of adopting a unilateral approach, patience and engagement remain far better tools with which to address the tribal areas.[22]

GENERAL ASSUMPTIONS AND IMPLICATIONS FOR U.S. POLICY

Accordingly, the first and most important baseline assumption of this report is that Washington will need to partner with leaders in Islamabad (and other Pakistani institutions) in order to accomplish U.S. goals in the tribal areas, despite the fact that Pakistan may lack the capacity—and at times, even the political will—to implement policies that serve these goals. Through a combination of structured inducements and patient investment in closer working relationships,

Washington should seek to win reciprocal Pakistani trust and confidence. Unilateral U.S. actions, whether military, political, or economic, are by no means proscribed, but their tactical benefits must be weighed against the potential costs they impose upon the broader goal of bilateral U.S.-Pakistan cooperation. Whenever possible, Washington should work with and through Islamabad.

Second, although the various terrorist, extremist, and militant groups operating in and near the tribal areas appear to have become far more interconnected (personally, ideologically, and operationally) since 2001, their distinctive motivations still offer cleavages to be exploited. Pakistani and U.S. counterinsurgency planners should identify and capitalize on the differences among international terrorists, foreign fighters, Afghan Taliban, Pakistani Taliban, and sectarian, tribal, and other violent groups. Even more important, extremist groups should be cut off from the general population as part of the Pakistani government's bid to reassert its legitimate, popular authority by demonstrating a capacity for good governance.[23]

Third, tactical security gains in the tribal areas, such as the defeat of a specific militant group or the elimination of a terror cell, will prove ephemeral if not complemented by rapid political change and economic incentives. In large swaths of the Pakistani-Afghan border region, the political economy now centers on militancy, crime, and smuggling, meaning that local moderates and representative (or traditional) leaders have no way of competing for positions of authority without assistance from the Pakistani government or other outside actors. By implication, Pakistan and the United States should seek to empower more moderate allies in the tribal areas by addressing their immediate political grievances and/or development needs.

Fourth, political and economic change cannot take place in an environment of extreme insecurity. The unprecedented levels of violence in some parts of the tribal areas must be addressed by military means before it makes sense to apply other nonmilitary tools. Accordingly, the development of Pakistan's capacity for counterterror and counterinsurgency missions is an essential priority that will require extensive, sustained financial and institutional investments by Washington and Islamabad.

Finally, transformative development programs that address the underlying causes of militancy, such as education and job creation, tend to be costly and take a long time. By implication, even the most successful U.S.-Pakistan partnership cannot fix the tribal areas overnight. This is truly a generational challenge—it must be recognized as such from the outset. Both American and Pakistani expectations should be appropriately calibrated, and institutional investments should be made to reflect the long-term commitment that will be required. Along the way, U.S. policymakers must also identify and track tangible measures of progress—even if incremental ones— so as to sustain political momentum despite the inevitable prospect of unanticipated challenges and unwelcome setbacks.

A Long-Term, Phased Approach

Given the challenges and assumptions above, the United States should address the tribal areas through a phased approach, with immediate, short-term, and long-term components. These phases suggest a policy roadmap but are not strictly intended to prioritize resources since long-term projects will require up-front attention and funding, and urgent security threats may crop up over an extended timeframe.

IMMEDIATE: MANAGE THE MOST URGENT SECURITY CRISES IN THE TRIBAL AREAS

For the United States, al-Qaeda is the single most urgent threat emanating from Pakistan's tribal areas because it is the only group with the demonstrated desire and capacity to strike the U.S. homeland. Taliban leadership and foot soldiers engaged in organizing and conducting attacks on U.S. and ISAF/NATO forces in Afghanistan represent the second-most-immediate threat. Pakistani militants (such as TTP and TNSM) are an immediate but primarily indirect threat, since they offer safe haven and support to other dangerous groups while simultaneously undermining the stability of the Pakistani state.

In the near term, these threats must be managed with existing political and military forces. Six primary tactics are available to these forces: targeted counterterror strikes, military offensives, border control, law enforcement, negotiations, and strategic communications. Since 2002, serious problems in the implementation of all six tactics have permitted—even contributed to—the breakdown of law and order in the tribal areas.

Counterterror Strikes

Targeted strikes against terror cells and militant commanders, including commando raids and the use of missiles fired from Predator unmanned aerial vehicles, will remain essential U.S. and Pakistani counterterror tools as long as al-Qaeda operates from remote regions that are otherwise inaccessible to large ground forces. Al-Qaeda's top leaders have proven remarkably elusive, and their global capacity to plan, fund, and inspire massive terrorist events makes their elimination an immediate imperative for Washington. Removing these individuals would offer the single most tangible sign of success in the fight against al-Qaeda, even if the organization were to carry on under new leadership.

That said, the political costs associated with these strikes must also be taken into consideration. Judging from press reports, the intelligence used to direct targeting remains imperfect; mistakes are inevitable. Civilians, including women and children, have been killed in these attacks, leading to popular protests against Pakistan's partnership with the United States. More than six years after 9/11, Pakistan's collective patience for counterterror efforts is thin. In many quarters, targeted strikes have been perceived as little more than American attempts to undercut peace negotiations between Pakistan's government and local militants.

With a new, more representative civilian government in Islamabad, the national debate over these counterterror tactics is likely to become more prominent and politicized than it was under Musharraf's military-led regime. A healthy debate might allow Pakistan to arrive at a more constructive national consensus on the need to combat militancy, but it simultaneously offers a chance for anti-U.S. critics to play up the costs of partnership.

The long-term costs of a bilateral rupture between Washington and Islamabad are likely to outweigh the potential gains from eliminating nearly any al-Qaeda leader. Decisions to eliminate specific terrorist cells must therefore be weighed against the plausible stresses they will impose on the U.S.-Pakistan partnership. This decision process would be enhanced by the creation of a forum for information exchange between senior U.S. and Pakistani national security officials.

Increasingly, another cost-benefit calculation must also be made, based on the fact that counterterrorism does not necessarily complement counterinsurgency. Counterterror operations that result in significant civilian casualties threaten to tip the scales of localized tribal sentiment against the Pakistani government. Militants have shown themselves to be quite shrewd in exploiting these attacks for propaganda purposes, uniting disparate groups under a common anti-Islamabad, anti-Western banner. Since a fundamental goal of counterinsurgency is to exploit differences between the different militant organizations and to drive a wedge between these groups and the wider population, the local costs of attacking any individual terror cell may outweigh the benefits. That said, in instances where operational links might have already been forged, such as between al-Qaeda and the TTP, hitting one should also hurt the other.

The choice to eliminate a terrorist or militant in Pakistan thus should involve more than a simple assessment of the direct threat he poses to the United States. In attempting to make the essential calculation about an attack's political implications, accurate information is paramount to success. Better pre-targeting intelligence can limit collateral damage and help policymakers determine whether local dynamics will make any given strike counterproductive in the context of a broader counterinsurgency mission.

Recommendations for U.S. policy include:
- Pakistan and the United States should establish a joint Security Coordination Committee. This committee, nominally chaired by U.S. and Pakistani national security advisers, would provide an institutionalized forum for consultation on the political dynamics associated with possible operations against terrorists and militant leaders. A new deputy cabinet-level coordinator for Pakistan and Afghanistan based at the State Department would oversee the committee's day-to-day operations.

– A working-level cell based in Islamabad and staffed by military and intelligence officers would support the joint Security Coordination Committee with intelligence sharing, strategies for crisis management, and longer-range planning. The committee would help national leaders avoid serious ruptures in the bilateral relationship and build greater confidence between the new civilian leaders of Pakistan and the U.S. government.

Military Offensives, Law and Order, Border Control, and Negotiations

In the immediate term, Pakistan's combined security, police, and intelligence services are manifestly incapable of eliminating militant groups in the tribal areas or stemming the flow of Taliban fighters across the Pakistani-Afghan border. The Pakistani army remains a blunt, conventional instrument with only rudimentary counterinsurgency capacity, better at inflicting punishing blows than targeting and eliminating specific enemies. Ongoing U.S. efforts to enhance FC and Pakistan army capacity through training and equipment will have only a minor impact over the next three years. A strategic stalemate in the tribal areas is the most realistic aspiration in this time frame.

Consequently, security and development efforts on the Afghan side of the border take on special urgency. Interdicting the narcotics trade is especially relevant. Without a more effective counternarcotics campaign in Afghanistan, one that stresses shutting down major trafficking rings, militants in Pakistan will continue to enjoy easy access to cash, and, by extension, to foot soldiers, vehicles, and weapons.

Driven primarily by recognition of its own weaknesses, the Pakistani government is likely to continue to pursue cease-fires and negotiated settlements in the FATA and NWFP. In Washington, evidence of the poor quality of security in Pakistan's tribal areas will inspire calls for unilateral military intervention and full-throated criticism of Pakistan's deal-making. But neither of these responses is constructive.

A unilateral U.S. intervention in Pakistan is not a serious option in any but the direst near-term scenario: a 9/11-type incident traced to terrorists operating from the tribal areas. In that event, Washington's leadership might feel compelled (by domestic politics and/or a desire to assert U.S. power) to undertake punitive bombing raids and ground incursions from bases in Afghanistan. But the U.S. military would find Pakistan's tribal areas extremely tough going. The primary challenge would come not from the militants or terrorists, but from the rest of Pakistan's 165 million people and army. Under almost any conceivable circumstance, the overwhelming majority of Pakistanis would perceive a U.S. invasion of the tribal areas as an attack on national sovereignty requiring resistance by every means possible. As a consequence, U.S. threats to unleash its military in Pakistan's tribal areas under less dire conditions lack credibility—they accomplish little other than to confirm Pakistan's worst suspicions about U.S. intentions.

Nor should Pakistan's negotiated settlements with local tribes be entirely written off. Tactically, cease-fires can offer a timely breather for Pakistan's overstressed army and other security services. Managed correctly, deals provide a means for the Pakistani government to divide its enemies from local populations (for instance, by seizing the moral high ground when militants violate the terms of an agreement), or to pit one set of militants against another. Therefore, Washington should avoid criticizing deals per se, but should certainly demand explanations about precisely how specific settlements are likely to benefit the counterinsurgents more than the insurgents. To the extent that Washington and Islamabad can agree on principles—or at least clarify U.S. redlines—for subsequent agreements, it would represent a tangible sign of progress.

Recommendations for U.S. policy include:
– In the near term, Washington should calibrate realistically its expectations for Pakistani security forces and must continue to

build capacity on the Afghan side of the border. Improving the Afghan security forces and pressuring the narcotics trade also weakens militants within Pakistan's tribal areas.

- The United States should refrain from threatening to intervene unilaterally and should not rule out the potential tactical utility of Pakistan's negotiations and cease-fires. Instead, Washington should clarify its specific preferences for future agreements, including a set of general principles (such as "accords should include a transparent mechanism for assessing infractions, action time lines should be announced publicly, tribal signatories must put up real property as collateral," etc.) and specific redlines (such as "no cross-border militancy, no safe passage or haven to foreign fighters, no participation in narcotics trade, no attacks on or obstruction of NATO/ISAF supply convoys for Afghanistan," etc.).

- Washington should stress Pakistan's sovereign responsibility to eliminate threats to international peace and security within its territory. This approach is important throughout the tribal areas, including Balochistan, where by most accounts Islamabad needs to take a more aggressive stance against resident leaders of the Afghan Taliban.

- To improve U.S. confidence in Pakistan's own military and to provide Washington with a greater window into the tactical logic of Pakistani army operations, the U.S.-Pakistan Defense Consultative Group (DCG) should hold meetings on a bimonthly basis, chaired by the new DC-based, deputy cabinet-level coordinator for Pakistan and Afghanistan, with participation from the Office of Defense Representative, Pakistan (ODRP).

- The ODRP should expand and constitute a new cell based in Peshawar to support the DCG and complement ongoing U.S. Embassy/ODRP activities in Islamabad. This new cell should partner with the Pakistani army, FC, and other security forces active in the tribal areas to obtain accurate, timely information on their operations.

Strategic Communications Gap

Pakistan's extremists demonstrate a remarkable capacity to exploit print and electronic media, undermining public faith in the government and security forces and building sympathy for anti-state causes. This is true throughout Pakistan, but is especially evident in the tribal areas, where mullah-run radio stations and DVD-based extremist propaganda unduly influence the local populace's opinion formation and appear to have played a central role in the rise of local militants, including Maulana Fazlullah in Swat Valley and Mangal Bagh in Khyber.

The Pakistani government has so far missed opportunities to influence the message. It has neither effectively presented its side of the story nor silenced the most egregious extremist propaganda. The military's approach to public relations has proven counterproductive in recent years. Because army spokesmen are typically unwilling to admit the deficiencies of their own institution, they tend to raise false expectations that ultimately leave Pakistanis (and international observers) frustrated and confused. In the present security stalemate, managing public expectations will be ever more essential to sustaining morale within the army's ranks and building confidence with Pakistani citizens. So while even the best communications strategy cannot overcome real deficits in the implementation or capacity of Pakistan's security forces, a poor strategy will unnecessarily exacerbate the challenge.

Recommendations for U.S. policy include:
- Drawing upon its strategic communications experience in Iraq and Afghanistan, the U.S. military should send advisers to the Pakistani security forces, including the army and FC.
- The United States should also offer to share relevant technical expertise in targeted FM radio broadcast jamming.

SHORT TERM: BRING RAPID, TANGIBLE POLITICAL REFORMS AND ECONOMIC OPPORTUNITIES TO WIN ALLIES IN THE TRIBAL AREAS

Genuine economic and political development is a long-term proposition. Even so, certain targeted efforts in the short term can reinforce immediate security gains and help to pave the way for more ambitious programming down the line.

Widespread political alienation and a dearth of lucrative, licit economic opportunities in the tribal areas fuel militancy in at least three ways. First, militant leaders win popular support by playing upon legitimate grievances with underperforming Pakistani government institutions, especially the judicial system and law enforcement in the provinces and the political agents in the FATA. Second, militants with income from smuggling, narcotics, and other illicit channels routinely intimidate or eliminate traditional tribal leaders who might otherwise ally with the Pakistani government. Third, poorly educated and unemployed young men in the tribal areas provide ready cannon fodder for insurgency in Pakistan and Afghanistan.

Redressing Grievances to Undercut Extremist Appeal: Law and Order

In NWFP and Balochistan, dysfunctional judicial systems and underpowered police forces stand out as examples of poor governance that contribute to widespread alienation. These institutions cannot be transformed overnight, but an immediate focus on reform and the rapid injection of resources could improve the situation in the short to medium term.

By many accounts, the popular appeal of sharia—a touchstone for militants like TNSM as well as Islamist political parties like JUI-F—is driven in large part by the breakdown of provincial judicial processes, notorious for extreme case backlogs. Rather than implementing sharia-based judicial systems and giving in to Islamist demands (as

advocated by the previous Muttahida Majlis-e-Amal government in
NWFP, or, even more recently, in the qazi-court proposals for the
PATA, which appear more symbolic than substantive), the Pakistani
government would gain greater credibility if it considered quick-
hitting reforms of the existing legal structures to grant relief to litigants
in cases that have dragged on for years.

Provincial police, often the first line of defense against militants in
NWFP and Balochistan, would benefit from better communication
and coordination with more heavily armed security services, including
the Frontier Constabulary and army.[24] In addition, the police need an
independent surge capacity in the form of rapid-reaction units—some
outfitted for SWAT-type operations, others to support larger-scale
investigations—in order to fill the gap between standard policing and
paramilitary operations.

Recommendations for U.S. policy include:
- The United States should assist Islamabad and Peshawar in
  formulating alternative strategies for judicial reform in the PATA,
  drawing upon technical expertise within the U.S. and Pakistani
  governments as well as international organizations.
- Washington should support (with funding and training) the
  expansion of a new provincial rapid-reaction police force, based on
  the recent NWFP proposal for 7,500 new officers with a "capital"
  cost of $70 million and an annual recurring cost of $15 million.[25]

Redressing Grievances to Undercut Extremist Appeal: Governance

In the FATA, a crisis of governance is likely to persist at least until the
tribal agencies are incorporated into modern, democratic institutions.
Recognition of this fact has led to calls for repeal of the FCR, which
would annul the colonial-era administrative framework that vests
political agents with supreme authority. But the risks to immediate

implementation of such a massive transition are quite high, particularly given the FATA's extremely poor security environment.

Three incremental reforms could help to redress legitimate political grievances without risking greater destabilization in the near term and would also pave the way for a more significant transformation over time.

First, extension of the Political Parties Act into the FATA could enable national political parties to compete for seats as they do throughout the rest of the country. This would begin the process of political normalization and integration.

Second, the FCR could be amended quickly to allow limited judicial appeal of decisions by political agents. Appeals could be heard by a special bench of the Peshawar High Court, but the specific process is less important than the broader implication: a limited right to appeal would empower legitimately aggrieved tribesmen and introduce a higher degree of responsibility among political agents without immediately destabilizing the existing administrative structure.

Third, a joint committee of the political agent and locally elected Agency Councils could make funding decisions for certain FATA development projects. At present, these councils have no defined purpose, but they might provide a representative consultative mechanism for more transparent distribution of resources and greater local ownership of development projects.

Recommendations for U.S. policy include:
- The United States should lend public support to FATA reform measures, including extension of the Political Parties Act and FCR amendment.
- In consultation with political agents, the NWFP High Court, and the Pakistani government, a U.S. advisory team should assist Pakistan in formulating proposals for a judicial appeals process in the FATA.
- USAID should identify a significant portion of FATA development assistance funding to be managed by committees that include

political agents and Agency Councils (or other local representative bodies). This process should begin with pilot studies in less violent agencies, then expanded over time.

Empowering Moderate Tribal Leaders

In addition to the longer-term humanitarian impact it might have, development assistance represents a valuable political incentive over the short run as an indirect means for building influence with and empowering local leaders. In the FATA, delivering resources to tribal leaders—in the form of cash or small development projects like schools, wells, or a visiting health clinic—might help them compete for public support against a new generation of militants. U.S. military commanders and USAID officers in Afghanistan and Iraq have funded smaller programs designed to have quick, tangible effects for similar tactical purposes.

At present, poor security conditions in the FATA will make the use of U.S. assistance to this end extremely difficult. Official U.S. activities are likely to be particularly constrained, given widespread and violent anti-Americanism as well as the concern that militants might specifically target U.S.-funded projects. In this context, it is essential that some development programs have the flexibility to reduce the local visibility of U.S. sponsorship ("branding") if necessary to achieve greater success on the ground.

The field offices of the political agents represent a unique platform for political, economic, intelligence, and military coordination in the FATA, backed by security from levies, the FC, and the Pakistani army. Despite the fact that these offices grant the political agents a great deal of influence and allow for relatively little U.S. influence or oversight, they provide the best near-term method for assistance delivery and regular interaction with tribal leaders.

Recommendations for U.S. policy include:

- In the short term, USAID should employ quick impact programming as a political tool to build inroads with tribal leaders. The relative profile of U.S. sponsorship for these projects should be calibrated to local security conditions. To the extent that existing legal restrictions limit USAID's flexibility (requiring extensive waiver procedures, for instance), Congress should consider legislative relief.
- Unless security conditions improve enough to facilitate official U.S. travel in the FATA, USAID should enhance its "virtual" forward presence by investing in communications technologies (secure internet, video, phone) to link up with field offices of Pakistan's political agents, thereby facilitating greater interaction with tribal leaders.
- Other technological tools should be considered to improve USAID's capacity for monitoring and oversight of its programs in remote locations, but Congress should also recognize the need for flexibility in instances where high-quality oversight is impossible but the political utility of development funds is clear.

Employing Young Men

USAID's $300 million Livelihoods Development Program includes a "cash-for-work" component, presumably intended to offer the young men of the FATA a nonviolent employment option.[26] Along with vocational training and investments in local industries, temporary work programs might well represent the first step toward salvaging parts of the region from a militancy-based economy. In the short run, a temporary work program may also be a useful means to compete with the Taliban for the many mercenary foot soldiers who only fight for the paycheck.

That said, any cash-for-work program that does not lead to stable, sustainable incomes might quickly prove counterproductive by frustrating the ambitions of the men (and their families) it is intended to serve. A successful program must be widely perceived as offering a realistic pathway out of poverty. But given the current lack of private-sector opportunities in the FATA, the Pakistani government may need to stand in as the primary employer in the near term. The FC, already a major public-sector recruiter from the FATA, could be expanded to include a civilian wing, commanded by army officers with expertise in relevant fields such as logistics, engineering, and management. Although such an effort might distract from the FC's other responsibilities, there are no other government institutions of consequence in the FATA to form the backbone of a civilian corps. Success will therefore require a commitment by the army to staff effectively both the military and civilian side of the FC.

This sort of civil service model offers at least two additional benefits: it would give the state a chance to forge greater economic links (and eventually trust) with tribesmen, and it would offer qualified, disciplined tribesmen an entry point for training and higher government service.

One recommendation for U.S. policy is:
- The United States should approach the FC, FATA Secretariat, and Islamabad to assist in establishing and maintaining a civilian wing of the FC as the cash-for-work component of its Livelihoods Development Program. Success should be measured by how quickly the program gets off the ground as well as the number of Pakistani tribesmen it employs in full-time, sustainable positions.

MEDIUM- TO LONG-TERM SECURITY: BUILD A SUSTAINABLE PAKISTANI COUNTERTERROR AND COUNTERINSURGENCY CAPACITY

While the United States and Pakistan seek to address immediate threats, they must also focus attention and resources on building Pakistan's independent capacity for fighting terrorists and militants over the medium to long run. More effective Pakistani military, police, and intelligence forces are necessary but insufficient ingredients for ultimate success.

In addition, Washington must overcome at least three high hurdles. First, Pakistan's security institutions will fail at counterinsurgency as long as they are not popularly perceived to serve a legitimate government. Second, the U.S.-Pakistan relationship is marred by deep distrust. Most Pakistanis continue to doubt U.S. commitment to the partnership, and a persistent sense of national insecurity, particularly with respect to India, continues to animate Pakistan's sluggish approach to shutting down all militant and extremist organizations. Third, Pakistan's progress is intimately connected to the ongoing struggle in Afghanistan, but strategies, institutions, and policies remain poorly coordinated across the Durand Line.

Building More Effective Security Forces

Significant U.S. resources—whether Coalition Support Funds, Foreign Military Financing, or other allocations for training and equipment—will be required to assist Pakistan's own security forces over the long haul. But more critical than the specific level of U.S. expenditures will be the process of transforming the organizational culture of Pakistan's security institutions. They need to evolve from stovepiped, bureaucratic structures designed to manage conventional wars and law enforcement operations into responsive, horizontally integrated units built to address a rapidly shifting spectrum of twenty-first century threats.

In the tribal areas, the army, FC, police, and intelligence services need to be networked and, where possible, operationally integrated. The Pakistani army will need to take the lead in this process, as it is the most well trained, disciplined, and financed. The army should develop and promulgate a new doctrine for counterinsurgency warfare and the United States should be ready to help. Army training and acquisition must reflect a serious and sustained commitment to this new mission, which cannot be handled by more commando units or a more robust FC alone. In short, the army must take full ownership of security in the tribal areas rather than perceiving the mission as a distraction from other responsibilities.

Several major hurdles stand in the way of U.S. efforts to build a more effective FC. The first is timing: even a minimal counterinsurgency capacity is difficult to develop and must be expected to take at least three to five years. Terrorists and militant groups will undoubtedly exploit this gap if it is not plugged by the Pakistani army. Second, although the Pashtun identity of FC troops should eventually make them better at navigating FATA's complicated political environment, in the near term, the FC's tribal allegiances may hurt morale and undermine effectiveness. Finally, the FC now lacks the capacity for tactical air support or mobility, leaving its troops especially vulnerable in difficult terrain.

Accordingly, short-term efforts to train and equip the FC are vital, but instead of building an FC with independent tactical air, intelligence, or logistical capabilities, the FC should be more fully integrated into the army. Only thorough integration can break down existing barriers to improved FC morale and effectiveness. The cultural, organizational, and technical barriers to integration must not be underestimated—the change will take time—but it will ultimately avoid duplication of effort and will help to keep the army engaged in the mission. Similarly, the development of rapid-reaction police units (in the provinces) and levies (in the FATA) are necessary steps, but cannot substitute for enhanced coordination with paramilitary and intelligence institutions.

Deep institutional, doctrinal, and operational changes to a nation's military never come easily, even in comparatively wealthy countries like the United States. Armies resist downsizing or reducing the prestige of once-dominant units—such changes require generational shifts in order to be implemented fully.[27] Washington can help to spur Pakistan's emphasis on the counterinsurgency mission by structuring U.S. military assistance in ways that reward transformation and discourage investment in conventional platforms.

Recommendations for U.S. policy include:
- The United States should use the DCG to help the Pakistani army develop a long-term commitment to counterinsurgency, which should include a road map for greater coordination and integration of the various security forces in the tribal areas.
- The United States should continue to provide significant security assistance to Pakistan, but the Pentagon should focus on equipment and training that will promote doctrine, training, and platforms appropriate for counterterror and counterinsurgency. Washington and Islamabad should begin by formulating a formal, jointly defined definition of U.S. assistance that emphasizes these categories.
- As an incentive to promote the army's long-term transition, to build capacity for countermilitancy, and to improve coordination with the FC, Washington should assist Pakistan in a major upgrade of its helicopter fleet. This upgrade should be phased in gradually, and be contingent upon the army's implementation of counterinsurgency doctrine and greater operational coordination with the FC.

Enhancing the Legitimacy of Force

Over the past year of electoral campaigns and political transition in Pakistan, a great deal of lip service has been given to the vital link between Pakistan's civilian political institutions and its long-term capacity to fight extremism and militancy.[28] In a nutshell, broader public debate is widely believed to represent the only means by which the Pakistani public might come to see the fight against extremism and militancy as its own—rather than America's—war. The fundamental weakness of Islamabad's military-led regime was its inability to legitimize its operations through a democratic process.

The electoral process that culminated on February 18, 2008, returned Pakistan's major political parties to power, but the relative balance of power between civilian and military institutions is still very much in flux. Given the historically dominant stature of the army, its political influence is not likely to wane quickly. At present, a civilian attempt to knock the army from its pedestal is probably more likely to hasten the return of a general as president than to prompt the army's meek retreat to its barracks.

A healthy civil-military balance would still accord the army a role in the formulation of security policy while subordinating its role in national leadership to civilian masters. Pakistan has rarely, if ever, achieved such a balance. Treating most of the various pathologies that plague Pakistan's civil-military relationship is well beyond the power of U.S. diplomacy or assistance. But a greater focus on the institutional structures charged with coordinating Pakistan's national security process would be a good place for Washington to start. President Musharraf's attempt to implement a National Security Council (NSC) was incomplete, under-institutionalized, and unlikely to last in its present form. Its successor institution might play an important role in improving working relations between politicians and officers, and, by extension, imparting greater democratic legitimacy to the military's activities. Regular meetings of this new body would represent near-term progress on the path toward civil-military reform.

Along with new institutional structures, Washington should invest in Pakistan's new national and provincial civilian leaders in order to help them increase their capacity for delivering improved services (health, education, infrastructure) and, by extension, for staving off extremist challengers. In addition, because Washington's close association with recent military regimes in Islamabad has convinced many Pakistanis that the United States prefers pliant generals over fractious civilians, the next administration would do well to counter these false perceptions by demonstrating a higher than normal degree of patience and generosity toward Pakistan's democratically-elected leaders.

Recommendations for U.S. policy include:
- In the context of a fluid, post-February 18, 2008, restructuring in Islamabad, Washington should use diplomatic pressure and technical assistance to support the establishment of an improved NSC-like institution, charged with facilitating communication and

coordination between Pakistan's civilian, defense, and intelligence agencies. If Islamabad rejects direct U.S. assistance on this sensitive issue, Washington should encourage other states with successful models of civil-military relations to play a more active role.

- To signal U.S. support for Pakistan's civilian leadership in Islamabad and the provincial assemblies, the next White House should work with Congress to win bipartisan support for multiyear assistance guarantees at a baseline no less than the levels delivered under the Bush administration. To build greater Pakistani trust in U.S. intentions, any conditions imposed on this assistance should focus on ensuring proper accounting procedures and building a closer working relationship between Pakistani and U.S. civilian officials.

Building Bilateral Confidence

In order for the U.S.-Pakistan security partnership to prove effective over the long haul, greater trust must be established on both sides at all working levels. In Pakistan, deep concerns about U.S. abandonment and a popular perception that the United States is simply exploiting Islamabad to serve its own purposes fuel resentment in military and civilian circles. Fears of Indian regional hegemony also make Islamabad particularly sensitive to Washington's improving relationship with New Delhi. Within Pakistan's army and intelligence services, the bilateral trust deficit is most acute in the junior and mid ranks, where personal interaction between Pakistanis and Americans is remarkably infrequent and where officers are most likely to reflect the anti-Americanism that dominates the national discourse.

In U.S. policymaking circles, a widespread concern that Pakistan may be hedging its bets by continuing to support militants passively (or actively) in order to project Pakistani power in the neighborhood fosters misgivings about the wisdom of increased security assistance. The policy often advocated by Americans most worried about Pakistani intentions is to threaten sanctions unless Pakistan demonstrates adequate commitment to prosecuting the fight against terrorists. But this approach risks backfire: threats to curtail U.S. assistance undermine Pakistani confidence in the bilateral partnership, raising insecurity and consequently rendering Islamabad even more likely to hedge its bets on militancy. This "confidence dilemma" is especially acute within the Pakistani military and intelligence communities, which are professionally inclined to prepare for worst-case scenarios.

Recommendations for U.S. policy include:

- In an effort to win the confidence of Pakistan's military, Washington should extend long-term security assistance guarantees at a baseline no less than the levels delivered under the Bush administration. And in order to demonstrate its intention for a lasting partnership, the next White House should seek a bipartisan congressional consensus for a multiyear package.

- Any conditions imposed on U.S. assistance—by the new administration or by Congress—should focus on processes designed to enhance bilateral confidence, such as mandating closer working relationships, greater information sharing, or more extensive joint training exercises, thus extending the U.S. "coercive embrace" of Pakistan rather than implying an underlying threat of abandonment.

- The ODRP should maintain a two-star presence in Islamabad. ODRP staffing should be expanded to enable greater liaison with Pakistani commands in Islamabad/Rawalpindi and Peshawar and to build greater transparency into the security relationship.

- To address Pakistani concerns about the U.S.-India relationship, Washington should support and facilitate India-Pakistan normalization efforts (primarily behind closed doors in New Delhi), and it should continue to brief Islamabad at the DCG regarding U.S.-India cooperation in a good faith effort to mitigate apprehensions despite obvious Pakistani preconceptions.

Pakistan-Afghanistan Coordination

Security in Pakistan's tribal areas depends upon security in Afghanistan and vice versa, but the only political-military institution that effectively spans the border is the Taliban. The Tripartite Commission and new Border Coordination Centers represent an attempt to fill this gap, mainly by providing venues for intelligence sharing and coordination at the strategic and tactical levels.

But in most ways Pakistan-Afghanistan confidence building remains in its infancy. Recent summit meetings and the Pakistan-Afghanistan peace jirga have been more symbolic gestures than tangible steps forward, in part because they have lacked persistent institutional support structures. Far more extensive steps are needed to integrate counterinsurgency operations, implement sophisticated border controls, and build a foundation for a sustainable reduction in bilateral tensions.

Many of the changes needed to achieve progress are politically sensitive and will require subtle diplomacy by motivated parties in both Kabul and Islamabad. The central dispute between Pakistan and Afghanistan—the Durand Line—cannot be negotiated to full mutual satisfaction because neither side can afford to face the firestorm of domestic political abuse that would follow territorial concessions. Increased bilateral interaction should be promoted without the expectation of political breakthrough, but with the hope that new discussion forums can drain tension from the broader relationship.

Other medium-term improvements in Pakistan-Afghanistan coordination might be facilitated by eliminating bureaucratic stovepipes that now exist within the U.S. government and NATO. For instance, inside the American National Security Council, Pakistan and Afghanistan are handled by different directorates, and there is no senior U.S. official with primary interagency responsibility for Pakistan-Afghanistan affairs. NATO maintains no institutional presence in Pakistan, despite the fact that the Afghanistan mission is the most ambitious deployment in the history of the alliance.

Recommendations for U.S. policy include:

- The United States should support the establishment of a Pakistan-Afghanistan peace secretariat with a headquarters and permanent binational staff as a means to build upon irregular bilateral summits and jirgas. A subcommittee of this secretariat could—on mutually acceptable terms—discuss technical border issues without necessarily attempting to resolve the Durand Line dispute.
- Within the U.S. national security bureaucracy, interagency responsibility for Pakistan and Afghanistan should be managed by a single deputy cabinet-level coordinator based at the State Department in order to seize opportunities for building connections across the two accounts.
- The new Pakistan-Afghanistan coordinator in Washington should draft a new National Security Presidential Directive that outlines U.S. strategy for addressing the threats of terrorism and militancy from Pakistan's tribal areas. An unclassified version of the strategy should be released in conjunction with a presidential speech on Pakistan policy within the first six months of 2009.
- The United States should press NATO's North Atlantic Council to open a diplomatic mission in Islamabad as a means to improve Brussels' capacity for cross-border analysis and planning.

MEDIUM- TO LONG-TERM POLITICAL/ECONOMIC: TRANSFORM PAKISTAN'S TRIBAL AREAS

Even a cursory review of the history of Pakistan's tribal areas exposes the fact that many of the most serious development challenges faced in 2008 have their origins in hundreds of years of history. That said, current political, economic, and social conditions also owe a great deal to more recent upheavals in Afghanistan, the global revolution in communications technologies, and what appears to be an irreversible breakdown in traditional tribal and administrative governing structures.

Therefore, regional development strategies must be informed by the past, but should not be aimed at a return to history. The region requires a fundamentally new political and economic rationale in order to escape from poverty and war. In the twenty-first century, threats like al-Qaeda dictate the need for the United States (and others) to support radical change in the FATA and throughout the Pakistani-Afghan tribal areas, including Afghanistan itself. A full transformation of this sort will take time, measured in decades or even generations, not budget cycles, and sustained by access to education, health care, and employment. It will require a new social contract between the people and the state, and the establishment of capable, modern institutions.

This vision for generational change should guide the U.S. and Pakistani approach to development even in the relative short term. Initial investments in political institutions and economic infrastructure may establish relationships and dependencies that are hard to break later. From this perspective, the issue of how best to incorporate the FATA into Pakistan takes on added significance. Similarly, the economic transformation of the tribal areas must begin with a realistic assessment of the region's possible comparative advantages in regional and global markets.

In order for Washington to support such a transition, it should also think realistically about its management of the business of assistance programming as well as the need to foster conditions more conducive to a sustainable U.S. development presence in Pakistan.

FATA Integration

The peculiar colonial-era mechanisms for governance in the FATA—its federal administration through the governor and political agents by application of the FCR—must yield to a more representative and transparent political process. But there are good reasons to avoid a rapid overhaul of the existing system. First, the demonstrated inability of the provincial government in NWFP to implement effective governance in the territories of the PATA raises questions about how well those same governance structures would cope with the even higher level of violence in the FATA. Second, scrapping the old system without an alternative in hand would likely lead to greater turmoil, and there is not yet a popular consensus about what a new political system should look like or how to implement it.[29]

Under these conditions, the office of the political agent may well remain a focal point for governance, even if it must be reformed and gradually morphed into a far different—more accountable, representative, and rule-of-law bound—sort of political institution. New frameworks for justice and state service delivery will need to be formulated, along with plans for taxation, utilities (electricity), and property laws.[30] Civil society groups, including Pakistani nongovernmental organizations (NGOs), will need to play a role in mobilizing and coordinating local sentiment on these issues.

Identifying the precise terms of this governance transition will first require the Pakistani government to undertake a broad process of consultation with tribesmen. For its part, U.S. investments in institutional capacity building should be harmonized with Pakistan's own reform plans.

Recommendations for U.S. policy include:

- The United States should press (and assist, where possible) the Pakistani government to plan and implement a formal mechanism for consultations between tribesmen and the government on a road map for political reform. One option for this mechanism would be to expand existing Agency Councils, though the expansion of the Political Parties Act might offer party-based alternatives. In agencies where security permits, the use of polling data to gauge public sentiment may also prove useful.
- USAID should develop capacity-building programs for the provincial governments of NWFP and Balochistan in order to improve service delivery and, if necessary, to prepare for the eventual provincial integration of the FATA.

Building an Economy

Relative isolation, few valuable natural resources, and difficult terrain pose serious challenges to growth in the tribal belt. It is no surprise, then, that raiding and smuggling have been the most profitable enterprises for centuries. Only a more highly skilled population connected to outside markets can possibly manage a better future.

Long-term economic prospects for much of the tribal areas hinge on regional land trade links, connecting markets and resources from Central to East Asia. Local trucking concessions are one area of the legal economy where Pashtun tribesmen have done extremely well. The greater the volume of trade, the more these businesses—and associated industries—will benefit. U.S. and other international donors already engaged in Afghanistan's development should also focus on this lifeline to the wider regional economy. The opening of the India-Pakistan border to trade and transit would likely provide the single greatest opportunity for a development boost along the land corridor through Pakistan into Afghanistan and Central Asia. The standardization of national tariff regimes throughout the region would also boost the flow of trade.

Prospects for industrial development in the FATA are dim in the short- to medium-term. But the relatively greater potential for building more business-friendly legal and administrative structures in the rest of the tribal areas (NWFP and Balochistan) suggests that supporting new industries on the fringes of the FATA may be the best medium-term approach to sustainable growth.

Balochistan's development prospects hinge on natural resources (especially gas) and the Gwadar port on the Arabian Sea, built with Chinese assistance. At present, both tend to contribute more to political tensions than to widespread economic opportunity. Many Baloch remain convinced that the profits from these investments will accrue to outsiders, deepening long-standing inequalities. Over the long run, Islamabad must address these political and economic grievances in order to stem the province's violently secessionist tendencies.

Few states or international donors other than the United States and Pakistan itself have responded generously to existing plans for development in the FATA. Major Pakistani partners, including China, Saudi Arabia, and the United Arab Emirates (UAE), have contributed remarkably little, considering the importance of Pakistan's national stability to these regions. If assistance and investment do start to accrue from a wider array of sources, avoiding duplication of effort will be essential. Given the complexity of harmonizing donor activities, the first priority for this group should be establishing baseline principles and sharing information on assistance programming throughout the tribal belt.

Recommendations for U.S. policy include:
- The United States and other international partners should include trade routes through Pakistan's tribal areas as an essential part of the regional development strategy for Afghanistan. The Regional Economic Cooperation Conference may be a useful forum for planning more ambitious strategies for investment and reforms that could boost land trade.
- Washington's proposed ROZs must be combined with infrastructure development programming to ensure the potential for profitability and the generation of employment opportunities for local populations. The opportunity to invest in ROZs and infrastructure improvements (roads, communications, water/ power supply) should be leveraged to attract additional outside investors from Pakistan and beyond.
- The United States should press Islamabad to formulate a long-term political and economic development strategy for Balochistan, including proposals for financial/technical assistance from the United States and other foreign donors or investors.
- The United States should organize a multilateral donor or investor group—including China, Saudi Arabia, the UAE, Japan, and the European Union—to improve coordination, transparency, and conditionality of assistance to Pakistan.

The Business of Development

As Washington contemplates the long-term expenditure of billions of dollars in development assistance for Pakistan's tribal areas, it must also consider whether existing bureaucratic practices are appropriate to the mission. As is the case throughout the world, USAID depends upon implementing partners—grantees and contractors—to manage projects. This business model offers global flexibility, and on average it may be more cost-effective than direct U.S. management by government personnel.

But if Washington intends to sustain development programming in Pakistan for at least the next decade, building USAID's in-house capacity may prove a better bargain if it enhances U.S. capacity for direct oversight and control. Moreover, a significant investment in U.S. personnel also demonstrates a more serious commitment to the many Pakistanis who are inclined to question U.S. staying power.

A long-term commitment to Pakistan (and Afghanistan) should therefore be matched by the creation of dedicated bureaucratic structures within the U.S. State Department and USAID, facilitated, if necessary, by congressional approval of specific waiver authorities. Managing programs of this magnitude and duration requires special personnel and procedures that may not be appropriate to the broader parent institutions with global responsibilities. In particular, the U.S. Foreign Service's standard practice of personnel rotation is inappropriate to the mission in Pakistan and Afghanistan. The accumulation of region-specific expertise is essential to success. The next White House may need to break with established bureaucratic practices in the Foreign Service in order to accomplish its long-term goals in this region.

But along with the ongoing, potentially accelerated expansion of U.S. presence in Pakistan, the United States must also seek ways to address the challenges of working in a political environment now dominated by anti-American sentiment. Where the delivery of development programming is more important than the fact that it comes from the generosity of American taxpayers, USAID should make efforts—as it has—to prioritize effectiveness over U.S. "branding." At the same time, in some cases, popular Pakistani expectations—based on Washington's promises of hundreds of millions of dollars in U.S. aid—would be better met with large-scale, high-profile U.S. projects. A proper balance must be struck between these two approaches.

Recommendations for U.S. policy include:
- The long-term U.S. commitment to all Pakistan's tribal areas (not limited to the FATA) requires specialized and expanded institutional structures and personnel, including a significantly larger embassy and consulate as well as supporting offices in Washington. The State Department and USAID should develop a professional corps of officers trained for service in Pakistan and Afghanistan.
- USAID should begin a process of transitioning from the use of "implementing partners" (contractors and grantees) to direct-hire officers in order to manage programs, build USAID's institutional memory and expertise, and demonstrate staying power to Pakistani partners. If necessary, Congress should pass legislation to facilitate these changes, specific to the Pakistan-Afghanistan context.
- USAID should identify and fund several high-profile, economically important development projects in the tribal belt, possibly in the power (electricity) or water management sectors, in addition to funding a wide variety of other programs that might benefit from a less prominent U.S. face.

Conclusion: Expanded, Long-Term U.S. Commitment Needed

The security challenges of Pakistan's tribal areas lie at the center of broader regional and global threats to stability. The best way to meet these challenges is through enhanced partnership with the political and security institutions of the Pakistani state, and the best way to improve this cooperation is by planning, organizing, and budgeting for a decades-long U.S. commitment to the region. Pakistan's recent history of turbulence and the threat of another 9/11-type attack provide a political impetus for significantly expanded action by the next White House.

The precise scale—in dollar terms—of U.S. assistance in Pakistan is not addressed in this report because the next administration should first undertake its own review of Pakistan's civilian and security requirements. This sort of review would represent a healthy corrective from recent practice. Washington's commitments to Pakistan after 9/11—President Bush's five-year $3 billion package and the recent five-year $750 million pledge for the FATA—were driven by political and diplomatic concerns, not prior U.S. needs-based assessments. That said, in the context of building a stronger bilateral partnership, the next administration must also bear in mind the symbolic and political significance of fulfilling prior commitments to Islamabad. This report therefore recommends that the Bush administration's pledges of $600 million per year (half civilian, half military) should serve as a baseline for new commitments. Additional funding may be needed to support the short- and long-term goals outlined throughout this report, from strengthening governance to building security institutions that are capable of a full range of counterinsurgency and counterterror missions.

The most urgent expansion of U.S. resources should come in the form of U.S. personnel and institutions built to uphold a long-term partnership with, and presence in, Pakistan. New investments are particularly vital on the civilian side (State and USAID) in order to expand, train, and maintain a cadre of experienced officers focused on developing programs for the tribal areas. Washington's political commitment will be best demonstrated and served by professionals who are encouraged to see the region as a career path rather than an exotic tour of one or two years. These improvements will require new expenditures in order to attract and retain talented individuals. They will also require the reform of existing bureaucratic personnel structures that now dissuade U.S. officials from focusing on the region in a sustained way.

Success in the approach recommended in this report should be judged by the strength of the U.S.-Pakistan partnership, as well as by the extent to which Pakistan demonstrates a commitment to making good use of resources—its own and those offered by Washington—in building an independent capacity for counterterror and counterinsurgency efforts. On both counts, Washington needs patience, as the necessary transformation of the tribal areas will require a generation or longer.

But U.S. patience must also have limits. Even though a complete transformation might take decades, incremental progress is required in order to sustain momentum in the bilateral partnership. The present political stalemate consuming Islamabad has divided and distracted Pakistan's civilian leaders. Unsurprisingly, the army has been reluctant to take particularly aggressive steps on its own, preferring a more passive role in the context of political uncertainty. Should Islamabad's drift persist well into 2009, the White House will be severely handicapped—robust cooperation requires at least minimal leadership and energy on the Pakistani side. Under these conditions, the next administration may need to consider alternative approaches toward Islamabad.

One such alternative, a U.S.-Pakistan relationship based on coercive sanctions—as opposed to one founded upon deeper partnership and U.S. incentives—could conceivably provide an effective stopgap against the most urgent threats to U.S. security. In many ways, Washington's approach toward Islamabad since 9/11 has combined the threat of sanctions with an oft-repeated commitment to long-term partnership. To date, the mix has been imperfectly calibrated, driven in part by jockeying between the Bush administration and Congress as well as among various agencies and departments of the executive branch. In the future, Washington could pursue a more precise policy of doling out incentives to (or threatening sanctions against) Pakistan's army and political leadership in return for meeting explicit U.S. demands, such as the elimination of specific terrorist cells, the mitigation of cross-border attacks into Afghanistan, or the permission to launch U.S. Predator strikes against targets on Pakistan's side of the border. In a narrow sense, this balancing of U.S. carrots and sticks would likely prove less costly in dollar terms than the more ambitious agenda outlined in this report.

The main problem with a future of coercive sanctions is that it would do little to treat the underlying causes of terrorism in Pakistan and even less to improve the tenor of the broader bilateral relationship. Since the weaknesses of Pakistan's political and security institutions already leave its society vulnerable to extremism and militancy, a U.S. policy that fails to build the capacity of the Pakistani state runs the risk that the state will deteriorate further and be captured by extremists. Imposing sanctions (or threatening them) also ignores Pakistan's capacity deficit in the near term. This deficit makes it more likely that U.S. demands will go unmet and, in turn, that bilateral tensions will increase. In short, U.S. coercion without Pakistani capacity or confidence is a recipe for aggravating frictions that could eventually destroy the relationship.

Another alternative to partnership with Pakistan would be for Washington to distance itself from Islamabad and to address specific security threats unilaterally or by building closer ties with other regional players. Rather than pressing Pakistan to act against al-Qaeda,

Taliban, and other militant groups operating within its territory, the United States would devote more effort to helping Afghanistan and India seal their borders, strengthening Kabul's independent capacity for security and governance, and developing the intelligence necessary to support U.S. counterterror attacks within Pakistan (whether by Predator strikes, limited ground incursions, or other means). Instead of undertaking an ambitious—and costly—partnership to transform Pakistan's military and civilian institutions, this approach would aim to cordon off the destabilizing influences of networks within Pakistan and to eliminate the worst terrorists and militants whenever possible. Washington's diplomats would then respond to the political fallout—in Pakistan and beyond—that would inevitably result from unilateral U.S. strikes on Pakistani soil.

But pulling away from Pakistan would impose significant costs. As with coercive sanctions, the United States would fail to address the underlying causes of instability and insecurity in Pakistan. In addition, without Pakistani partnership the United States (and NATO/ISAF) would need to find a new way to supply its mission in Afghanistan. At present, no Central Asian alternative exists to the Pakistan-based logistics hub, at least not one capable of supporting operations at the current (or an expanded) tempo. Even more troubling, over time Washington's decision to pull away from Islamabad coupled with unilateral U.S. military incursions into Pakistan's tribal areas would likely yield a further deterioration in the bilateral relationship, spiraling downwards to frosty tension or even hostility.

If U.S.-Pakistan relations do crumble—if Pakistan's future leaders choose to ride a wave of populist anti-Americanism, fail to take steps toward transforming military and civilian institutions, and rekindle support to extremist organizations in the face of Washington's protests—then a U.S. strategy of containment and deterrence would be in order. Under these conditions, the United States would seek to limit Pakistan's reach beyond its borders, threaten overwhelming retaliatory strikes to deter Pakistani hostility, and shore up Pakistan's neighbors in the region, particularly Afghanistan and India. A U.S. shift toward containment would also entail political and economic coercion to isolate Pakistan and reduce its access to dangerous technologies and resources.

But a U.S. containment and deterrence policy would deliver only marginal guarantees of security. Containment and deterrence are more effective against unitary states with recognized leadership hierarchies and institutions than against hard-to-find, secretive, subnational organizations (like al-Qaeda or its successors) that would likely pose the greatest security threats from Pakistan. Without Islamabad's cooperation, Washington would have significant trouble tracking and impeding the movement of terrorists within or through Pakistan. And U.S. deterrent threats of massive retaliation against the territory or people of Pakistan would only work if the Pakistani state itself has the capacity to police the activities of militants and terrorists on its soil. An Islamabad further weakened by U.S. containment would have no such control.

THE LEAST WORST OPTION

Investing in a long-term partnership with Islamabad will not be cheap or easy. But the foreseeable costs associated with all of the realistic alternatives are even more daunting. The next occupant of the White House should keep these costs in mind if the frustrations of working with and through Islamabad mount and patience with the partnership grows thin.

As a global superpower, the United States is far better placed than Pakistan to bear the burden of even these suboptimal outcomes. This sobering reality, in combination with the tangible benefits Pakistanis would gain from a cooperative, long-term partnership, may well inspire at least some of Pakistan's leaders to welcome the comprehensive strategy advocated by this report and to encourage a reciprocal approach by Islamabad.

Appendix: Summary of Recommendations

STRATEGIC SHIFT: FORMALIZE DIRECTIVES AND REFOCUS BUREAUCRACY

Within Six Months:
- Designate a new deputy cabinet-level coordinator for Pakistan-Afghanistan and task him or her to draft a National Security Presidential Directive for Pakistan's tribal areas. Release an unclassified version of this strategy document in conjunction with a presidential speech.

Medium-to-Long Term:
- Build the United States' capacity for maintaining a sustained commitment to Pakistan's tribal areas by investing in expanded institutions and specialized personnel, particularly within the State Department, the U.S. Agency for International Development, and the Office of Defense Representative, Pakistan.

BILATERAL POLICY: INTENSIFY PARTNERSHIP WITH PAKISTAN AND BUILD CAPACITY

Within a Year:
- Establish a new U.S.-Pakistan Joint Security Coordination Committee to improve bilateral confidence and information sharing on political dynamics related to the tribal areas.
- Convene bimonthly meetings of the U.S.-Pakistan Defense Consultative Group to improve military-military cooperation.

- Publicly express support for basic reform measures in Pakistan's Federally Administered Tribal Areas, including the extension of the Political Parties Act and amendment of the Frontier Crimes Regulation.
- Provide advisers to assist Pakistan's strategic communications effort.
- Clarify U.S. objectives and specific redlines for Pakistani negotiations with tribal leaders.

Medium-to-Long Term:
- Task the DGC to develop a road map for greater coordination and integration of the various Pakistani security forces in the tribal areas.
- Enhance USAID's "virtual" forward presence in the FATA by investing in communications technologies to connect with the field offices of Pakistan's political agents.
- Establish a civilian conservation corps for the FATA.
- Press for, and support, efforts by the Pakistani government to implement a mechanism for consultations between tribesmen and the government regarding a road map for political reform in the FATA. Work with Islamabad and provincial governments to formulate alternative strategies to reform the judiciary and improve the government's capacity to deliver services throughout the tribal areas, and press Islamabad to formulate a long-term development plan for Balochistan.
- Support the formation of a new National Security Council–like institution in Islamabad charged with enhancing coordination between civilian, defense, and intelligence agencies.
- Multilateral Policy: Coordinate with Other Concerned States
- Within a Year:
- Propose that the NATO's North Atlantic Council should open a diplomatic mission in Islamabad.
- Facilitate India-Pakistan normalization efforts through quiet diplomacy, and use more frequent meetings of the DCG to brief Islamabad on the character of U.S.-India cooperation efforts.

Medium-to-Long Term:
- Organize a multilateral donor/investor group, including China, Saudi Arabia, the United Arab Emirates, Japan, and the European Union to improve coordination, transparency, and conditionality of assistance to Pakistan.
- Support a permanent Pakistan-Afghanistan peace secretariat with a headquarters and binational staff.
- Develop plans for enhanced land trade between South and Central Asia with outreach to members of the Regional Economic Cooperation Conference on Afghanistan.
- Resources: Treat Pakistan's Tribal Areas as a Top-Tier National Security Threat
- Within a Year:
- Following strategic review and budgetary assessment, seek bipartisan congressional approval for long-term assistance guarantees to Pakistan for both military and civilian programming at or above existing levels.
- Employ quick impact programming as a political tool to establish inroads with tribal leaders in the FATA.

Medium-to-Long Term:
- Assist the expansion of a new provincial rapid-reaction police force in the North-West Frontier Province.
- Identify and fund high-profile "U.S.-Pakistan Friendship" development projects in the tribal areas as well as a variety of other projects with less prominent U.S. "branding."
- Press ahead with U.S. Reconstruction Opportunity Zones only if combined with infrastructure development projects to enhance profitability and to ensure that tribal populations benefit from the new economic opportunities.
- Expand U.S. military assistance on equipment and training to bolster the Pakistani army's commitment to counterterror and counterinsurgency missions.

- Promote counterinsurgency capacity and coordination between Pakistan's army and Frontier Corps units by offering to assist in the stand up of a new, integrated helicopter fleet.

About the Author

Daniel Markey is a senior fellow for India, Pakistan, and South Asia at the Council on Foreign Relations. From 2003 to 2007, he held the South Asia portfolio on the policy planning staff at the U.S. Department of State. His responsibilities included analysis and planning for the secretary of state on regional and global policy issues, participation in departmental and interagency South Asia policy formulation, articulation of regional policy for senior-level speeches and print media, and acting as a liaison with academic, think tank, and diplomatic communities.

Prior to government service, Dr. Markey taught at Princeton University and served as the executive director of Princeton's Research Program in International Security. In 2000 and 2001, he was a postdoctoral fellow at Harvard University's Olin Institute for Strategic Studies. He received a BA in international studies from Johns Hopkins University and a PhD from Princeton University's Department of Politics.

Advisory Committee for
Securing Pakistan's Tribal Belt

Note: Council Special Reports reflect the judgments and recommendations of the author(s). They do not necessarily represent the views of members of the advisory committee, whose involvement in no way should be interpreted as an endorsement of the report by either themselves or the organizations with which they are affiliated.

Mission Statement of the
Center for Preventive Action

The Center for Preventive Action seeks to help prevent, defuse, or resolve deadly conflicts around the world and to expand the body of knowledge on conflict prevention. It does so by creating a forum in which representatives of governments, international organizations, nongovernmental organizations, corporations, and civil society can gather to develop operational and timely strategies for promoting peace in specific conflict situations. The center focuses on conflicts in countries or regions that affect U.S. interests, but may be otherwise overlooked; where prevention appears possible; and when the resources of the Council on Foreign Relations can make a difference.

The center does this by:

- *Convening Independent Preventive Action Commissions* composed of Council members, staff, and other experts. The commissions devise a practical, actionable conflict-prevention strategy tailored to the facts of the particular conflict.
- *Issuing Council Special Reports* to evaluate and respond rapidly to developing conflict situations and formulate timely, concrete policy recommendations that the U.S. government, international community, and local actors can use to limit the potential for deadly violence.
- *Engaging the U.S. government and news media* in conflict prevention efforts. The center's staff and commission members meet with administration officials and members of Congress to brief on

CPA's findings and recommendations; facilitate contacts between U.S. officials and critical local and external actors; and raise awareness among journalists of potential flashpoints around the globe.

- *Building networks with international organizations and institutions* to complement and leverage the Council's established influence in the U.S. policy arena and increase the impact of CPA's recommendations.
- *Providing a source of expertise on conflict prevention* to include research, case studies, and lessons learned from past conflicts that policymakers and private citizens can use to prevent or mitigate future deadly conflicts.

Center for Preventive Action
Advisory Committee

John W. Vessey Jr., USA
General, USA (Ret.); Chair, CPA Advisory Committee

Morton I. Abramowitz
The Century Foundation

Peter Ackerman
Rockport Capital Inc.

Patrick M. Byrne
Overstock.com

Antonia Handler Chayes
Tufts University

Leslie H. Gelb
Council on Foreign Relations

Joachim Gfoeller Jr.
GMG Capital Partners, L.P.

Richard N. Haass
Council on Foreign Relations

David A. Hamburg
Cornell University Medical College

John G. Heimann
Financial Stability Institute

George A. Joulwan
General, USA (Ret.); One Team, Inc.

Jane Holl Lute
United Nations

Vincent A. Mai
AEA Investors Inc.

Margaret Farris Mudd
Financial Services Volunteer Corps

Kenneth Roth
Human Rights Watch

Barnett R. Rubin
New York University

Robert G. Wilmers
Manufacturers & Traders Trust Co.

James D. Zirin
Sidley Austin LLP

Council Special Reports

Sponsored by the Council on Foreign Relations

Avoiding Transfers to Torture
Ashley S. Deeks; CSR No. 35, June 2008

Global FDI Policy: Correcting a Protectionist Drift
David M. Marchick and Matthew J. Slaughter; CSR No. 34, June 2008

Dealing with Damascus: Seeking a Greater Return on U.S.-Syria Relations
Mona Yacoubian, Scott Lasensky; CSR No. 33, June 2008
A Center for Preventive Action Report

Climate Change and National Security: An Agenda for Action
Joshua W. Busby; CSR No. 32, November 2007
A Maurice R. Greenberg Center for Geoeconomic Studies Report

Planning for a Post-Mugabe Zimbabwe
Michelle D. Gavin; CSR No. 31, October 2007
A Center for Preventive Action Report

The Case for Wage Insurance
Robert J. LaLonde; CSR No. 30, September 2007
A Maurice R. Greenberg Center for Geoeconomic Studies Report

Reform of the International Monetary Fund
Peter B. Kenen; CSR No. 29, May 2007
A Maurice R. Greenberg Center for Geoeconomic Studies Report

Nuclear Energy: Balancing Benefits and Risks
Charles D. Ferguson; CSR No. 28, April 2007

Nigeria: Elections and Continuing Challenges
Robert I. Rotberg; CSR No. 27, April 2007
A Center for Preventive Action Report

The Economic Logic of Illegal Immigration
Gordon H. Hanson; CSR No. 26, April 2007
A Maurice R. Greenberg Center for Geoeconomic Studies Report

The United States and the WTO Dispute Settlement System
Robert Z. Lawrence; CSR No. 25, March 2007
A Maurice R. Greenberg Center for Geoeconomic Studies Report

Bolivia on the Brink
Eduardo A. Gamarra; CSR No. 24, February 2007
A Center for Preventive Action Report

After the Surge: The Case for U.S. Military Disengagement from Iraq
Steven N. Simon; CSR No. 23, February 2007

Darfur and Beyond: What Is Needed to Prevent Mass Atrocities
Lee Feinstein; CSR No. 22, January 2007

Avoiding Conflict in the Horn of Africa: U.S. Policy Toward Ethiopia and Eritrea
Terrence Lyons; CSR No. 21, December 2006
A Center for Preventive Action Report

Living with Hugo: U.S. Policy Toward Hugo Chávez's Venezuela
Richard Lapper; CSR No. 20, November 2006
A Center for Preventive Action Report

Reforming U.S. Patent Policy: Getting the Incentives Right
Keith E. Maskus; CSR No. 19, November 2006
A Maurice R. Greenberg Center for Geoeconomic Studies Report

Foreign Investment and National Security: Getting the Balance Right
Alan P. Larson, David M. Marchick; CSR No. 18, July 2006
A Maurice R. Greenberg Center for Geoeconomic Studies Report

Challenges for a Postelection Mexico: Issues for U.S. Policy
Pamela K. Starr; CSR No. 17, June 2006 (web-only release) and November 2006

U.S.-India Nuclear Cooperation: A Strategy for Moving Forward
Michael A. Levi and Charles D. Ferguson; CSR No. 16, June 2006

Generating Momentum for a New Era in U.S.-Turkey Relations
Steven A. Cook and Elizabeth Sherwood-Randall; CSR No. 15, June 2006

Peace in Papua: Widening a Window of Opportunity
Blair A. King; CSR No. 14, March 2006
A Center for Preventive Action Report

Neglected Defense: Mobilizing the Private Sector to Support Homeland Security
Stephen E. Flynn and Daniel B. Prieto; CSR No. 13, March 2006

Afghanistan's Uncertain Transition From Turmoil to Normalcy
Barnett R. Rubin; CSR No. 12, March 2006
A Center for Preventive Action Report

Preventing Catastrophic Nuclear Terrorism
Charles D. Ferguson; CSR No. 11, March 2006

Getting Serious About the Twin Deficits
Menzie D. Chinn; CSR No. 10, September 2005
A Maurice R. Greenberg Center for Geoeconomic Studies Report

Both Sides of the Aisle: A Call for Bipartisan Foreign Policy
Nancy E. Roman; CSR No. 9, September 2005

Forgotten Intervention? What the United States Needs to Do in the Western Balkans
Amelia Branczik and William L. Nash; CSR No. 8, June 2005
A Center for Preventive Action Report

A New Beginning: Strategies for a More Fruitful Dialogue with the Muslim World
Craig Charney and Nicole Yakatan; CSR No. 7, May 2005

Power-Sharing in Iraq
David L. Phillips; CSR No. 6, April 2005
A Center for Preventive Action Report

Giving Meaning to "Never Again": Seeking an Effective Response to the Crisis in Darfur and Beyond
Cheryl O. Igiri and Princeton N. Lyman; CSR No. 5, September 2004

Freedom, Prosperity, and Security: The G8 Partnership with Africa: Sea Island 2004 and Beyond
J. Brian Atwood, Robert S. Browne, and Princeton N. Lyman; CSR No. 4, May 2004

Addressing the HIV/AIDS Pandemic: A U.S. Global AIDS Strategy for the Long Term
Daniel M. Fox and Princeton N. Lyman; CSR No. 3, May 2004
Cosponsored with the Milbank Memorial Fund

Challenges for a Post-Election Philippines
Catharin E. Dalpino; CSR No. 2, May 2004
A Center for Preventive Action Report

Stability, Security, and Sovereignty in the Republic of Georgia
David L. Phillips; CSR No. 1, January 2004
A Center for Preventive Action Report

Endnotes

[1] For more on this issue, see Stephen P. Cohen, *The Idea of Pakistan* (Washington, DC: Brookings Institution Press, 2004); Frederic Grare, *Rethinking Western Strategies Toward Pakistan: An Action Agenda for the United States and Europe* (Washington, DC: Carnegie Endowment for International Peace, 2007); Husain Haqqani, *Pakistan: Between Mosque and Military* (Washington, DC: Carnegie Endowment for International Peace, 2005); Daniel Markey, "A False Choice in Pakistan," *Foreign Affairs*, vol. 86, no. 4 (July/August 2007), pp. 85–102; Ashley J. Tellis, *Pakistan and the War on Terror: Conflicted Goals, Compromised Performance* (Washington, DC: Carnegie Endowment for International Peace, 2008).

[2] For general background on Pakistan's tribal areas, this report draws from International Crisis Group, *Pakistan's Tribal Areas: Appeasing the Militants*, December 11, 2006; Thomas H. Johnson and M. Chris Mason, "No Sign Until the Burst of Fire," International Security, vol. 32, no. 4 (Spring 2008), pp. 41–77; Noor ul Haq, et al., "Federally Administered Tribal Areas of Pakistan," IPRI Paper 10, March 2005, http://www.ipripak.org/papers/federally.shtml; Naveed Ahmad Shinwari, "Understanding FATA: Attitudes Toward Governance, Religion & Society in Pakistan's Federally Administered Tribal Areas" (Peshawar: Community Appraisal & Motivation Programme, 2008), available at http://understandingfata.org/report 20pdf.html; Akbar S. Ahmed, Social and Economic Change in the Tribal Areas, 1972–1976 (Karachi: Oxford University Press, 1977); Khalid Aziz, "Causes of Rebellion in Waziristan," Regional Institute of Policy Research and Training Peshawar Policy Report, February 22, 2007; Government of Pakistan, *FATA Sustainable Development Plan 2007–2015*, available at http://www.worldsecuritynetwork.com/documents/Booklet_on_FATA_SDP_2006_-_15.pdf.

[3] Johnson and Mason, "No Sign Until the Burst of Fire," p. 62; Akbar Ahmed, *Social and Economic Change in the Tribal Areas, 1972–1976*, p. 16.

[4] For a discussion of the army's resistance to change, see Tellis, *Pakistan and the War on Terror: Conflicted Goals, Compromised Performance*, p. 24.

[5] Shinwari, *Understanding FATA*, p. 70.

[6] For more on transitional strategies in Pakistan's tribal areas, informed by the British colonial experience in India, see Joshua T. White, "The Shape of Frontier Rule: Debating Governance from the Raj to the Modern Pakistani Frontier," *Asian Security*, vol. 4, no. 3 (Autumn 2008), forthcoming.

[7] See Government of Pakistan, *FATA Sustainable Development Plan 2007–2015*.

[8] See quotes from former Interior Minister Aftab Sherpao in Saeed Shah and Jonathan S. Landay, "Pakistan Military Started Talks with Islamists," McClatchy Newspapers, April 30, 2008.

[9] See press release, P.R. no. 226, Prime Minister's Secretariat, June 25, 2008, available at http://www.pid.gov.pk/press25-06-08.htm.

[10] "National Intelligence Estimate: The Terrorist Threat to the U.S. Homeland," National Intelligence Council, July 17, 2007; Central Intelligence Agency (CIA) Director Michael V. Hayden, "Interview by Tim Russert on Meet the Press," NBC News, March 30, 2008.

[11] David Rohde, "Foreign Fighters of Harsher Bent Bolster Taliban," *New York Times*, October 30, 2007.

[12] For more on TTP, see Hassan Abbas, "A Profile of Tehrik-i-Taliban Pakistan," *CTC Sentinel*, vol. 1, no. 2 (January 2008).

[13] For more, see Frederic Grare, *Pakistan: The Resurgence of Baloch Nationalism* (Washington, DC: Carnegie Endowment for International Peace, 2006).

[14] For more on the links between militancy and madrassas in Pakistan, see International Crisis Group, *Pakistan: Madrasas, Extremism and the Military*, July 29, 2002; Tahir Andrabi et al., "Religious School Enrollment in Pakistan: A Look at the Data," *John F. Kennedy School of Government Working Paper*, no. RWP05-024, March 2005; Saleem H. Ali, *Islam and Education: Conflict and Conformity in Pakistan and Beyond* (Karachi: Oxford University Press Pakistan, forthcoming); and C. Christine Fair, "Militant Recruitment in Pakistan: A New Look at the Militancy-Madrasah Connection," *Asia Policy*, vol. 1, no. 4 (July 2007).

[15] U.S. Department of Defense, *Report in Response to Section 1232(A) of the National Defense Authorization Act of Fiscal Year 2008*, 110th Cong., 2nd sess., March 2008, p. 11.

[16] On the Federal Bureau of Investigation and CIA role in apprehending terrorists in Pakistan, see Zahid Hussain, *Frontline Pakistan: The Struggle With Militant Islam* (New York: Columbia University Press, 2007), pp. 125–127; On a recent border violation, see Carlotta Gall and Eric Schmitt, "Pakistan Angry as Strike by U.S. Kills 11 Soldiers," *New York Times*, June 12, 2008; For recent reports on alleged U.S. Predator strikes, see Joby Warrick and Robin Wright, "Unilateral Strike Called a Model For U.S. Operations in Pakistan," *Washington Post*, February 19, 2008; Eric Schmitt and David E. Sanger, "Pakistan Shift Could Curtail Drone Strikes," *New York Times*, February 22, 2008; Robin Wright and Joby Warrick, "U.S. Steps Up Unilateral Strikes in Pakistan," *Washington Post*, March 27, 2008; Mark Mazzetti and Eric Schmitt, "U.S. Military Seeks to Widen Pakistan Raids," *New York Times*, April 20, 2008. Noteworthy attacks in Pakistan attributed to the use of Predators include May 2005, North Waziristan, Haitham al-Yemeni killed; January 13, 2006, Damadola, eighteen civilians killed; October 30, 2006, Chingai; January 31, 2008, North Waziristan, Abu Laith al-Libi killed; May 14, 2008, Damadola, Abu Suleiman al Jaziery reportedly killed.

[17] Government Accountability Office, *Preliminary Observations on the Use and Oversight of U.S. Coalition Support Funds Provided to Pakistan*, GAO-08-735R, May 6, 2008.

[18] Security-related aid ran to $7.833 billion from 2002 to 2008. See K. Alan Kronstadt, "Direct Overt U.S. Aid and Military Reimbursements to Pakistan, FY2002–FY2009," Congressional Research Service, May 9, 2008.

[19] Afghanistan and Pakistan Reconstruction Opportunity Zones Act of 2008 was introduced in the Senate on March 13, 2008, and in the House on June 26, 2008.

[20] On British contributions, see Simon Cameron-Moore, "U.S. Aims to Turn Hostile Pakistani Tribes Friendly," Reuters, January 30, 2008, "Pakistan Wants UK Aid to Develop Tribal Areas: PM," *Daily Times*, April 8, 2008, and "Britain Doubles Aid to Pakistan," BBC News, July 3, 2008, available at http://news.bbc.co.uk/2/hi/south_asia/7486948.stm. On Japanese contributions, see Mariana Baabar, "Japan To Help Develop Tribal Areas," *The News*, May 4, 2008.

[21] See http://www.terrorfreetomorrow.org/upimagestft/PakistanPollReportJune08.pdf, pp. 28–29.

[22] The term "conflicted ally" is from Ashley J. Tellis, "Pakistan—Conflicted Ally in the War on Terror," Policy Brief no. 56, Carnegie Endowment for International Peace, November 2007.

[23] On the centrality of asserting government legitimacy and capacity in counterinsurgency, see *The U.S. Army/Marine Corps Counterinsurgency Field Manual* (Chicago: University of Chicago Press, 2007), pp. 170–173, 235.

[24] For more on Pakistan's internal security, see C. Christine Fair and Peter Chalk, *Fortifying Pakistan: The Role of U.S. Internal Security Assistance* (Washington, DC: U.S. Institute of Peace Press, 2006).

[25] Figures confirmed by Pakistani law enforcement official.

[26] USAID, *FATA Development Program*, January–March 2008, April 14, 2008.

[27] On the difficulty of innovation in military institutions, see Stephen Peter Rosen, *Winning the Next War: Innovation and the Modern Military* (Ithaca, NY: Cornell University Press, 1991), pp. 2–3.

[28] See Benazir Bhutto, "When I Return to Pakistan," *Washington Post*, September 20, 2007; Grare, *Rethinking Western Strategies Toward Pakistan: An Action Agenda for the United States and Europe* (Washington, DC: Carnegie Endowment for International Peace, 2007), p. 7; Husain Haqqani, "Terror vs. Democracy in Pakistan," *Wall Street Journal*, October 25, 2007.

[29] The only recent attempt to survey the FATA's residents provides strong evidence of a lack of consensus. See Shinwari, *Understanding FATA*, pp. 88–90.

[30] For more on the traditional formulas for allocation of tribal incomes (such as rents from government or private entities), see Stephen Alan Rittenberg, *Ethnicity, Nationalism, and the Pakhtuns: The Independence Movement in India's North-West Frontier Province* (Durham, NC: Carolina Academic Press, 1988), pp. 31–33.

www.ingramcontent.com/pod-product-compliance
Lightning Source LLC
Chambersburg PA
CBHW050549280326
41933CB00011B/1776